Making Sense of a Suffering World

The Bible and a Life Story Reveal Answers to Why God Allows Suffering

KEN DIGNAN

WestBow
PRESS
A DIVISION OF THOMAS NELSON

T0369040

WestBow Press books may be ordered through booksellers
or by contacting:

WestBow Press
A Division of Thomas Nelson
1663 Liberty Drive
Bloomington, IN 47403
www.westbowpress.com
1-(866) 928-1240

ISBN: 978-1-4497-9285-5 (sc)
ISBN: 978-1-4497-9286-2 (hc)
ISBN: 978-1-4497-9284-8 (e)

Library of Congress Control Number: 2013907313

Printed in the United States of America.

WestBow Press rev. date: 09/09/2013

Ken Dignan is a fellow journeyman on the path marked with suffering—our disabilities have given us both a seasoned perspective on the goodness of God and the problem of affliction. His love for Christ, respect for God's Word, and passion to share biblical encouragement is truly admirable!

—Joni Eareckson Tada, Joni and Friends
International Disability Center

As a young preacher's kid growing up in the suburbs of Chicago, I first knew Ken simply as one of my dad's closest friends in the ministry. My brothers and I grew up with his sons and shared many wonderful times together. I watched and was inspired by a man who overcame more than his fair share of life's obstacles all with a smile on his face and joy that was felt by all he came in contact with. Ken has continued to inspire me ever since those early days as I have been a personal witness to his faith in the midst of trials and suffering. With his new book, I believe that once again God is going to use Ken's story and his powerful perspective to reach many hurting people who are struggling to make sense of it all.

—Matthew West, national recording artist,
singer/songwriter

Ken's story is an amazing journey of triumph through tragedy. I've never met someone who was able to have such joy through such pain. But to find *purpose* in suffering takes incredible depth. It's much better to learn through our suffering. Ken will help you do just that.

—Tim Harlow, senior pastor, Parkview Christian
Church, Orland Park, Illinois; top 100 largest and
fastest-growing churches in America, according to
Outreach Magazine and Lifeway Research.

Table of Contents

Acknowledgments vii
Introduction...ix

Chapter 1: Knocking on Heaven's Door.....................1
Chapter 2: Why, God? 20
Chapter 3: Establishing a Theology About Suffering... 38
Chapter 4: The Value of Suffering 64
Chapter 5: Not Home Yet.....................................85
Chapter 6: The Meaning of True Happiness 111
Chapter 7: Looking Back 133
Chapter 8: A Life-Changing Experience................. 153
Chapter 9: Don't Waste Your Suffering 177
Chapter 10: Arriving Home.................................. 208
Chapter 11: A Glimpse of Heaven 228
Chapter 12: The Hierarchy of Heaven and
            Activities Beyond 258

References to quotes 279
Discussion Questions and Reflections—
Chapter by Chapter 285
Scriptures Used-Chapter by Chapter 293
Recommended Reading 297
Recommended Song List for Inspiration................. 299
About the Author.. 301

Acknowledgments

I desire to acknowledge the education and the schools that have allowed me to lay a firm theological foundation. I received a bachelor's degree (B.A.) in Bible and pastoral theology from North Central University in Minneapolis, Minnesota; and a master's degree (M.A.) in biblical studies, plus extra credits towards a master's of divinity degree (M.Div.) from the Assemblies of God Theological Seminary, in Springfield, Missouri.

I appreciate and acknowledge the many churches where I've held pastoral positions: Maranatha Chapel in Evergreen Park, Illinois, youth and Christian education pastor; First Assembly of God in Jerseyville, Illinois, youth and assistant pastor; Living Water Community Church in Bolingbrook, Illinois, senior pastor (led two building programs); the Stone Church, in Orland Park, Illinois, assistant pastor; and Eagle Rock Community Church, Homer Glen, Illinois, senior pastor and various assistant pastor roles. Along with pastoring I've served as an evangelist and the founding president and director of 'Til Healing Comes Ministries. These have all enriched my life with the many relationships developed and countless hours spent in counseling and study for sermons, teachings, conferences, retreats, and seminars.

This book is dedicated in love and appreciation to my family, who has influenced my life greatly: my wife, Joni; my four sons, Andy (and his wife, Jodi, and daughters Riley and Kara); Patrick (and his wife, Jennifer); Britt; and the late Ryan (September 15, 1980-December 14, 2002).

I also dedicate this to my parents, the late Leo (January 28, 1928-March 8, 2011) and Rosemary Dignan; my five brothers (Steve, Ray, Don, Leo, and Marty) and three sisters (Julie, Rosemary, and the late Jean, July 10, 1957-January 6, 1974) along with their spouses and children; and all my friends too numerous to name.

Special thanks to my wife, Joni, and my personal assistant, Jeanna St. Louis, for assisting with editing. I also appreciate my brother Steve Dignan and John Koys who is married to my cousin Patricia (Dignan), for reading my manuscript and offering their comments and suggestions.

Introduction

Suffering has been my bedfellow as far back as I can remember. I am unable to recall a day in my life where I didn't have some type of pain or suffering. Physical problems and suffering have been part and parcel of my life since I contracted the polio virus when I was only fourteen months old. It was three years before the mass distribution of the Salk vaccine that began to make this dreaded disease obsolete.

I'm sure if you could go to the beginning of human history, mankind has wrestled with many questions: Why is there so much suffering in this life? Why do bad things happen to good people and good things happen to bad people? If God is so good, how could He allow evil to exist? How can you say God will not give you more than you can handle?

Lee Strobel, a noted Christian pastor, author, scholar, and lecturer, sent out a questionnaire asking, "If you could ask God just one question, what would it be?" The number one response was, "Why does God allow so much suffering and evil?"

I will be giving answers to this question, experientially and theologically. I share many of the lessons learned from a lifetime of suffering. I relate various personal stories from numerous experiences disclosing what I've had to suffer, while drawing parallels to Scripture and theology. My ultimate goal is communicating practical, down-to-earth answers for this all-important topic of suffering.

There are foundational truths laid down in the Bible that have guided biblical scholars and theologians to establish building blocks for the faith. We live in a broken world, a place where man's free will caused him to sin. Thus a perfect world became corrupted.

God had a backup plan already established to offer redemption and salvation to mankind through the sacrificial death of Jesus Christ. He came to Earth, born of the Virgin Mary to become the suffering messianic Lamb of God. Herein lies the focal point of history, which revolves around the death, burial, and resurrection of Christ.

You may know you are a genuine follower of Christ. You may call yourself a Christian and be unaware of exactly what that means, or possibly you're not sure where you stand with your beliefs.

I have written this book to lay out an apologetic, which is a defense of the faith, for those who believe in God and the Bible, to help them come to a clearer understanding of why God allows suffering.

However, if you are unsure about your faith or are convinced that there is no God, I hope you will gain a better understanding of what the Bible teaches on the subject and reconsider faith in God as a viable part of your life.

Even though I have a disability from polio, the Lord has helped me accomplish many things for His glory. I was raised in an excellent home atmosphere where my parents raised me to believe in God, have faith, and not allow my disability to keep me from following my dreams, drives, or desires.

I am highly motivated to share my personal life stories and my knowledge of the Bible. A passage in Psalm 105:1-5 encourages believers to share what God has done in their lives:

> Oh give thanks to the LORD, call upon His name; Make known His deeds among the peoples. Sing to Him, sing praises to Him; Speak of all His wonders. Glory in His holy name; Let the heart of those who seek the LORD be glad. Seek the LORD and His strength; seek His face continually. Remember His wonders which He has done, His marvels and the judgments uttered by His mouth.

Disability doesn't mean "no ability." In fact it's been said, "The only true disability in life is a negative attitude." I have what I call a "believe attitude," which comes from my belief in God. By faith in God and His Word, I pursued many passions in my life, and have not been prohibited or limited by the physical challenges the wicked polio virus left me. God has graciously given me a tremendous number of blessings and talents, as well as a tremendous amount of inner strength. I truly know what it means to have good times and bad times, blue skies and gray skies, sunny days and rainy days.

God has helped me reach many milestones, including these:

I've been married to my best friend and wife for more than thirty-five years, have raised four unbelievable sons, and been blessed with wonderful daughters-in-law and two grandchildren.

I've earned a college and postgraduate degree to prepare me for pastoral ministry along with the teaching of scripture and theology; founded 'Til Healing Comes Ministries; produced and hosted a contemporary Christian music radio program in the St. Louis area; produced and hosted a weekly Christian television program that was seen all over the Chicago area and on many cable stations throughout the United States and the world.

I've organized and promoted an annual concert and fund-raiser for the awareness and prevention of suicide with such artists as Sanctus Real, Tenth Avenue North, Matthew West, Jimmy Needham, Josh Wilson, and Seventh Day Slumber, along with leading a Survivors of Suicide support group for a number of years to help families cope with and grieve the loss of a loved one, especially a teenager or young adult.

I've been a musician, able to play the drums, acoustic guitar, electric guitar, and bass guitar, and I've recorded a CD of contemporary gospel songs and worship choruses.

I've authored the books *'Til Healing Comes* and *Ryan's Story.*

I've definitely experienced these two Scripture verses: Matthew 19:26, which says, "With God all things are possible;" and Philippians 4:13, which says, "I can do all things through Christ who strengthens me."

Perhaps your life has been filled with suffering. If it hasn't, count your blessings, because the reality is, suffering comes as a normal experience everyone will have to face at one time or another. It's how you approach the suffering that will make or break you.

You may say, "It's not fair. Why did this have to happen to me? I can't ever catch a break. I might as well give up. My life will never get better."

You can get angry. You can yell at God and call Him unfair and uncaring. You can take it out on those closest to you.

You might become withdrawn and quiet, hiding from the outside world and those who care about you. You can turn off the lights, close the curtains, pull the blankets over your head, and cry, "Woe is me."

I encourage you to embrace your suffering. Accept that it happens and is a natural part of life. Realize that much of the time spent on this planet has to do with suffering.

The goal of this book is to help you understand and make the most out of your times of hurt and pain. God uses suffering as a powerful tool to develop character, compassion, humility, faith, and perseverance, and even to prepare you for how you may serve God in heaven. It is my prayer that you will be encouraged, enlightened, and educated so you can make sense out of why God allows suffering.

Get ready to discover the vast scriptural details in the lives of the biblical characters, the truths God revealed to them in the Bible that deal with suffering and what they were inspired to say about their trials and tribulations.

Along with that, you'll see the way suffering has influenced my perspective and how my faith in God and His Word has prepared me to live a blessed and productive life that even brought me to "knocking on heaven's door."

CHAPTER 1

Knocking on Heaven's Door

I t was New Year's Eve, December 31, 2011. I became extremely sleepy early in the afternoon. I was at home that Saturday and told my wife I was going to take a nap.

I was in my motorized scooter, which I used every day to get around because of my disability. Its seat was comfortable enough for me to lay back, rest my head, and go to sleep.

It became no ordinary nap. Somehow I fell into a deep sleep. A half hour went by and then an hour passed, but I slept on. I had been struggling with tiredness during the day for a number of months. It wasn't unusual for me to take a catnap lasting maybe ten to fifteen minutes, usually later in the day.

Oddly, one of my brothers, Ray, who lived nearby, felt a strong desire to drive over to my home to visit me. It was a bit unusual for him to drop by unannounced, but he did.

Blindsided by a Nap

He rang the doorbell. My wife answered and he asked, "Is Ken around?"

She said, "Yes, but he's taking a nap."

He asked, "How long has he been sleeping?"

She responded after looking at the clock, "Boy, it's been over an hour or more."

My brother said, "Can we check in on him and wake him up?"

After entering, they found me fast asleep. "Time to wake up, Ken," Ray said jokingly. But I did not respond. He touched my shoulder and shook me a bit and said, "Ken, wake up. Hello. C'mon, Ken." I was still unresponsive. They continued trying to arouse me, but all their efforts failed.

My brother and wife realized something was seriously wrong. Instead of calling an ambulance, they decided to rush me to a nearby hospital. Ray jumped on the back of my scooter and drove it to the garage, down the ramp and into my disability minivan. The ramp to the van was lowered and he managed to direct the scooter into the vehicle. They got me situated and my brother got into the driver's seat.

Joni tried to hold me securely in the scooter while Ray rushed down the highway. That must have been a harrowing trip. I vaguely remember a momentary consciousness during that drive where I almost fell out of the scooter after a wild turn. Otherwise, I was still out of it, deeply groggy, mostly unconscious.

Thank God I was brought to the hospital successfully and rushed to the emergency room entrance. Upon my arrival, hospital staff got me out of the van, onto a gurney, and into an examination room.

Immediately, doctors saw that my oxygen levels were extremely low. They started me on oxygen while they took X-rays of my chest to look at my lungs.

I do not remember any of this. In fact, I do not recall many things about my first few days in the intensive care unit. All that happened is very hazy.

I begin this book about suffering to show that I am no stranger to it. I've often felt like and said, "Life doesn't seem fair." I've thought about the question, "Why does God allow suffering?" countless times as a polio survivor.

I have survived numerous major surgeries, illnesses, grief, and tragedies, along with chronic aches and pains. After this recent health scare, I thought deeply again about how a good and loving God could create a world filled with so much suffering, pain, and evil.

Regardless of the amount of suffering one may encounter and experience, it is still not easy to face new blows that will come.

Scrambling for a Diagnosis

Those blows kept coming as doctors scrambled furiously to figure out why I was unconscious and struggling to wake up. In and out of consciousness, I remember seeing the concern on the faces of my wife and family members. I thought, *What is going on? What's wrong with me? Am I going to die?*

I began to sense I might be on my way to see the Lord. As a genuine believer and follower of Christ for more than forty years, I lived assured and excited about the prospect of going to Heaven when I died. However, when confronted with the prospect of being at death's door and told by doctors I might not have much longer to live, I was a little less willing to say goodbye to family and friends.

Remarkably, I had a deep peace about the whole situation. Normally I was an anxious person when it came to being hospitalized, but the Lord was giving me a supernatural calm to accept His will, whatever it was.

Suffering from Various Symptoms

For more than twelve months prior to this hospitalization I had quite a few days when I did not feel well. During that time an over-night sleep study revealed I was struggling with a disorder called sleep apnea. I would get tired during the day and have trouble staying asleep at night. I had nightmares and vivid dreams, and I often talked in my sleep.

I was having problems regulating my body temperature, with regular readings between 97.5 and 95.6. Occasionally my temperature read as low as 92.5. Those who have had polio can be extremely sensitive to and intolerant of cold, but this was worrisome.

I was unable to taste anything, which really concerned me. I went to an ear, nose, and throat specialist to have my sense of taste, sinuses, and some hearing problems checked. He couldn't find any reason why I was unable to taste food.

I had visited a well-known university hospital in the downtown Chicago area, along with being hospitalized recently near my home. Still the doctors were unable to diagnose why this was happening.

Their vague response was that my symptoms were caused by post-polio syndrome. PPS is a recent diagnosis the medical community ascribes to certain symptomatic relapses of those who contracted the polio virus earlier in life, before the Salk vaccine. I had a feeling this problem was something other than post-polio.

An Assurance of God's Presence

However, here I was in the intensive care unit of a hospital in serious condition and I had an inner calm. I had an assurance that God was with me and that He was in control. I felt like I was doing what an old Bob Dylan song said: "Knock, knock, knockin' on Heaven's door." Remarkably there was a peace that encouraged me to feel I was ready to go and an acceptance of passing from Earth to glory.

I went in and out of consciousness several times. In between those moments it was almost as if I were in the very presence of God while in that deep sleep. I sensed that I was so close to being in Heaven, I could almost hear the singing of praise and worship before the Lord.

For a Christian, Life or Death Is a Victory

A passage I was familiar with, that God inspired the apostle Paul to write, came freshly to my mind and heart. It's found in Philippians 1:20-26.

> I eagerly expect and hope that I will in no way be ashamed, but will have sufficient courage so that now as always Christ will be exalted in my body, whether by life or by death. For to me, to live is Christ and to die is gain. If I am to go on living in the body, this will mean fruitful labor for me. Yet what shall I choose? I do not know! I am torn between the two: I desire to depart and be with Christ, which is better by far; but it is more necessary for you that I remain in the body. Convinced of this, I know that I will remain, and I will continue with all of you for your progress and joy in the faith, so that through my being with you again your boasting in Christ Jesus will abound on account of me.

Having taught and preached on this portion of Scripture many times, I knew all about what Paul was saying. Now I could actually echo these words for myself in the midst of my suffering.

Throughout my Christian life I prayed God would "be exalted in my body by life or death." With all I'd gone through thus far with a body that was devastated by the polio virus, I often wondered how much more I could take. In times of great suffering I thought, *Take me, Lord; I'm ready to go.* Then I'd pray, "But Lord, if You still desire me to, I'll stay here for Your glory as I continue to depend on Your power and strength."

I was encouraged by this passage again. I was able to share with my wife and family and tell them how much I loved them. I saw my siblings and their families, my nieces and nephews, and my eighty-three-year-old mother. Our father had passed on to heaven ten months earlier. It was a strange experience to see all those closest to me at my bedside, hugging me and crying.

My main concern was for Joni. I remember asking my sons and siblings, along with their spouses, to take care of my wife.

During this time I again received comfort from stories, passages, and verses in the Bible that seemed inwardly wrapped around my heart, mind, and soul. They exploded like fireworks on the Fourth of July in my thoughts, constantly sustaining and upholding me. You will see many of them sprinkled throughout this book.

I have regularly turned to the book of Job, which is found in the Scriptures, to receive insight and encouragement from one who went through a painful time of physical suffering, loss, and grief.

Suffering and the Book of Job

Old Testament scholars believe there is evidence that the book of Job may be one of the first stories put to parchment in the Bible. His story would predate Moses' recording of the stories revealed and passed down found in the book of Genesis. This means that God and suffering go a long way back.

Theologian and author Dr. Norman Geisler says, "Other than Genesis, Job is possibly the oldest book in the Old Testament. At the least the story is set in pre-Mosaic patriarchal times" (1).

We gain a behind-the-scenes look at why God allowed Job to suffer. The enemy of his soul, Satan, came to God questioning Job's reason for his faithfulness. Satan said the only reason Job trusted God was that the Lord gave him blessings and benefits.

God told Satan he was wrong. Satan then asked Him if He would remove His hedge of protection from Job and his family. Satan argued that Job would curse God and deny his faith if difficulties came his way. "The Lord said to Satan, 'Very well, then, everything he has is in your power, but on the man himself do not lay a finger'" (Job 1:12).

Enemies came and stole all his cattle. Fire fell from the skies and destroyed his grains, thus taking any provisions or worldly wealth. After that, Satan sent a storm that killed all his children, their spouses, and his grandchildren. Only he and his wife were spared, though Job was given painful sores all over his body.

Job had no clue, at the time, why all the tragedies were happening to him and his family. He didn't know he was caught in the middle of a disagreement between God and Satan.

His wife didn't even encourage him, and told him to give up: "His wife said to him, 'Are you still maintaining your integrity? Curse God and die!'" I'm sure she was going through great turmoil and agony at losing all her children and grandchildren. She apparently gave in to anger and doubt toward God.

Job's remarkable faith and trust in God kept shining through as he replied, "'You are talking like a foolish woman. Shall we accept good from God, and not trouble?' In all this, Job did not sin in what he said" (Job 2:9-10).

Thank God my wife has been supportive throughout my disability, illnesses, and rehabilitations.

The Bible records that Job did not deny his faith in God, nor did he curse the Lord. Read what he said after he received all the terrible news:

"At this, Job got up and tore his robe and shaved his head. Then he fell to the ground in worship and said: 'Naked I came from my mother's womb, and naked I will depart. The LORD gave and the LORD has taken away; may the name of the LORD be praised.' In all this, Job did not sin by charging God with wrong doing" (Job 1:20-22).

Job knew God was using his trials as a test to refine his faith and trust. After all his sufferings and pain he said, "Though He slay me, yet will I trust Him" (Job 13:15); "When He has tested me, I shall come forth as gold" (Job 23:10).

On top of all this he had three friends who came and chided him. They said he had surely done something wrong and sinned, causing God to allow all the troubles to occur in his life and family.

Even though they caused him great emotional pain, he forgave them. In fact, after he prayed for them, the Lord released more blessings in his life than he had before.

> After Job had prayed for his friends, the LORD restored his fortunes and gave him twice as much as he had before. All his brothers and sisters and everyone who had known him before came and ate with him in his house. They comforted and

consoled him over all the trouble the Lᴏʀᴅ had brought on him, and each one gave him a piece of silver and a gold ring.

The Lᴏʀᴅ blessed the latter part of Job's life more than the former part. He had fourteen thousand sheep, six thousand camels, a thousand yoke of oxen and a thousand donkeys. And he also had seven sons and three daughters ... Nowhere in all the land was there found women as beautiful as Job's daughters, and their father granted them an inheritance along with their brothers.

After this, Job lived a hundred and forty years; he saw his children and their children to the fourth generation. And so Job died an old man and full of years. (Job 42:10-17)

Granted, Job did suffer tragic losses and endure intense physical pain for many months. But after his great trial, God blessed him with great prosperity and many more offspring. He was able to live for 140 more years.

Occasionally during extra difficulties I've thought, *Boy, Lord, everybody looks at how much Job suffered, but what about me? I've been suffering for more than sixty years now. Can I get a double blessing too?*

I know this is not the kind of thinking or attitude God wants me to have. It is rare that these grumblings occur to me, but I must be on my guard. I continually depend on the Lord to help me face my suffering with His strength and grace.

Noted theologian Dr. R .C. Sproul said the following:

> The answer comes clearly from the wisdom of the book of Job that agrees with the other premises of the wisdom literature: the fear of the Lord, awe and reverence before God, is the beginning of wisdom. And when we are befuddled and confused by things that we cannot understand in this world, we look not for specific answers always to specific questions, but we look to know God in His holiness, in His righteousness, in His justice, and in His mercy. Therein is the wisdom that is found in the book of Job. (2)

I was going to need the type of faith Job exhibited to be able to recover and get through any rehabilitation. I earnestly desired to ultimately get home and have caregivers, family, and friends to help me. I kept praying, as did many others, that God would allow me to survive and get through this.

Suffering Can Cause Uncertainty About the Future

It was a constant battle to fight worry that my whole life's direction could change. I have been motivated to work in vocational ministry since I graduated from seminary in 1976. For more than thirty-five years my disability did not prohibit me from being able to work and provide for my family as I held a variety of pastoral positions.

I found myself wondering whether I would be able to fully recover to fulfill the responsibilities of my full-time pastoral ministry. I was thinking, *What if this latest calamity makes it necessary to step down and take a break from my position as a pastor? How long will I be in the hospital or a rehabilitation center?* I'd always known in my heart that I'd pursue some type of pastoral ministry, but I became anxious when I worried about my future too much. I had to keep committing my future to the Lord as a reminder that He had it under control.

Specialists suggested that if I recovered, I might need an extended time to recuperate. They recommended that I slow down and let up on my schedule to regain and maintain my health.

I was proud, in a good way, that I always had a job as a pastor that allowed me to earn a livable income and provide for my family, despite my disability all these years. But not knowing the actual direction my health could take was a genuine concern and matter of earnest prayer.

I really didn't want to step aside and resign from the church I loved, at which I had spent the last fourteen years of my life in ministry. However, I had no idea of the timetable for my recovery and if I would be able to keep up with the demanding schedule of the pastorate?

I knew I could never totally stop ministering and officially retire. I would always want to find ways to share the love of Christ along with being able to preach and teach the Bible, and minister in some way. I was thankful I had founded a nonprofit ministry I kept going simultaneously; it could always use my assistance.

Not knowing the future is a troublesome thing. I was battling for my health and my head was spinning, thinking about all these scenarios. Yet I had to make pertinent decisions as soon as possible.

Serving as a pastor has been a true blessing. I've thanked God for the opportunities to serve Him all my life. It has been the ideal calling and career that fit my disability well. Early in my Christian life I asked the Lord to use me.

I prayed a prayer that said, "Lord Jesus, I can't tie my own shoes, get myself dressed, or put my hand in my pocket to take out my wallet. But I give you my life, my mind, my heart, my soul, and my mouth for you to use me as you please." God graciously took me up on this prayer and I can't praise Him enough for blessing me in the ministry.

As hard as it would be, I reluctantly accepted that, under the circumstances, it would be wise to step down from my pastoral position at the church.

I was grateful to God for my miraculous recovery but I didn't how long it would take to get out of the rehabilitation center, or what my daily regimen would entail to maintain my health.

It was tough to finally tell the church about my decision. Deep down I had to trust that the Lord would lead me into whatever future ministry He had in store.

All this was swirling around me like a tornado while I continued praying and hoping I would survive and stay on the path of recovery. I saw that there were many twists and turns in the road ahead.

God Is the Great Orchestrator of Circumstances

I kept reflecting on well-loved Scriptures in the Bible, especially this one in Romans 8:28, which declares,

"And we know that in all things God works for the good of those who love him, who have been called according to his purpose."

This can be a challenging Scripture to believe and agree with when you're suffering a lot. I have to admit it is very difficult to accept the truth that God is at work in a believer's life when everything looks bad.

Throughout my Christian life I have found this verse to be a comfort. It's been tried, tested, and found true. Therefore I could confidently hold on to it throughout all my physical, emotional, and spiritual challenges.

I was close to Heaven, so close I could almost see it, touch it, and hear it. It's easy to think, *How can God get something good out of this?* Yet time and again those who follow Christ have seen good come out of bad, triumph come out of tragedy, and blessings come out of tremendous burdens.

I have definitely seen and experienced God turning negative situations into something positive for His glory. This truth was having a profound effect on the way I was handling this medical emergency.

In the midst of suffering and pain and the uncertainty of what would present itself next, I was able to keep my focus on the Lord and His perfect will. I knew, without a doubt, that God was in charge of my life and circumstances.

God had demonstrated to me that He is faithful and loving. I could rest my faith in the truth that whatever lay ahead in my path, God was looking out for my good. He was directing my steps.

Years ago I learned to rely on another portion of Scripture found in the book of Proverbs: "Trust in the LORD with all your heart and lean not on your own understanding; in all your ways submit to him, and he will make your paths straight" (Proverbs 3:5-6).

Even during a medical emergency, God is still in charge of what happens to His children. It is imperative for every Christian to trust in this promise whenever facing trials of any kind.

It is easy to lose sight of God's leading and direction in the time of an emergency. That's why it's beneficial for every believer to daily spend good times and not-so-good times reading and meditating on the Scriptures.

The Bible will prepare our lives for any challenges that may come our way. I like to look at it like feeding our soul in the same way we feed our bodies daily. We all know we should eat food each day to stay healthy.

In the same way we should feed our souls with the Word of God and prayer each day for spiritual nourishment. Jesus referred to it like this: "It is written: 'Man shall not live on bread alone, but by every word of God" (Luke 4:4 NKJV). God's Word is the "Bread of Life."

As you study the Bible, you will find answers to the questions of life. One major time when individuals look for answers is during times of physical difficulties. There are many answers for that number one question mankind has asked since the beginning: "Why, God?"

CHAPTER 2

Why, God?

Doctors continued to search for a diagnosis. They were still trying to figure out why I was unable to wake up and stay conscious.

More tests were taken such as magnetic resonance imaging, computed tomography scans, X-rays, blood draws, and more. The tests confirmed that my severe scoliosis did not allow my lungs the proper space they needed. Since my spine was seriously curved in many places, the lungs did not have the adequate space to function properly, so they operated at a much lower capacity.

I had known about that problem for a long time, even back in my late twenties. Years ago, respiratory care specialists put me through a battery of tests that revealed that my lung capacity was 25 percent. I had been able to live with that most of my life. Now doctors searched for why there were a number of complications developing that did not allow me to exhale enough carbon dioxide, causing it to build up in my bloodstream, affecting my oxygen levels.

They believed the muscles were weaker and the curvature of the spine, especially on my right side, collapsed on that lung and pressed on the lower part, not allowing it to move or function properly.

Adding to this, a sleep study revealed I would stop breathing a hundred times or more when I slept, which I hadn't realized. That more than likely was contributing to a carbon dioxide buildup that left me with symptoms of being very sleepy during the day, causing a lack of high-quality sleep.

My respiratory doctor said the best and major way to deal with sleep apnea was to use a mask that covered the nose and mouth and was hooked up with a hose to a bi-pap machine. It is more accurately called a BPAP (bi-level positive airway pressure) machine, a breathing apparatus that helps its user get more air into his or her lungs.

Seeing that I could not put my own mask on, I had not been using it or the machine at all before this emergency. Put this all together and you have a dangerous health risk that was one of the contributing factors that brought me to this place.

Seeing my oxygen count was low and the carbon dioxide levels were high, the staff in the Intensive Care Unit placed me on the bi-pap, hooking it up to oxygen.

The doctors did not know how I'd respond to treatments. A respiratory specialist said if I did not recover well enough, there was a good chance I'd need a tracheotomy and live on a ventilator machine. That didn't sound like an inviting kind of future. My family was trying to be as optimistic as possible even though the doctors were not painting a rosy picture.

I Didn't Look Too Good

Later, friends who visited me in the I.C.U. remarked that I looked dangerously ill. So ill that after they left my room, their conversation went along the lines of how much time it would be until I died. One of them said that he thought I'd be dead and in heaven within a few days.

Every day that went by meant I was responding to the treatments of oxygen and the bi-pap machine. They had me on a strong antibiotic in an IV. Doctors discovered and drained fluid from my lungs. Medical specialists believed they were doing all they could, and the rest would be up to the Lord.

I was still here on Earth this side of Heaven. My faith in God was giving me peace of mind, because I knew God was in charge. Even though I didn't know if I'd continue to recover, my faith in God was definitely sustaining me.

I had a lot of time lying there in the hospital to reflect on all the truths from Scripture that would reinforce my trust in God. Despite this, there was a constant battle with fear, worry, and questioning why this was happening.

Suffering Often Causes One to Say, "Why, God?"

It is frightening how one medical emergency can change the course of your life. There have been times, in my own humanness, when I have asked God, Why?— basically, Why do I have to suffer so much? I do not believe that asking why betrays or minimizes how deep your faith and trust in God is. It simply reveals you are human. It's what you do with this question that makes all the difference in the world.

I know with my head that the Bible has many answers for why there is so much suffering, pain, and evil in this world. However, with my heart I sometimes struggle with it.

I've accepted that there is more to this life than what we see. Scripture tells us that if we will listen to our soul and the depths of our heart, we'll hear, "Life doesn't end when we die on earth, and there is an afterlife." This helps one deal with life and death situations in a positive way.

I've enjoyed a few of the top clichés about dealing with challenges: "If life gives you lemons, make lemonade;" "Tough times will either make you bitter or better;" and finally, "Tough times don't last, but tough people do."

Positive sayings can be catchy, but they're not always easy to live by and apply. Many have a difficult time approaching suffering in a positive manner. Sadly, it's natural to allow suffering to cause anyone to question why, or doubt there is a God.

On the contrary, though, I believe asking why causes you to reason deep down, "God must exist." It shows there's a longing inside that senses something must have gone wrong. Something must have happened that brought suffering, pain, and evil into this world. The why can cause you to search for answers.

Intuitively, man knows something went wrong with this world. The only sensible explanation is found in the Bible. The Scriptures tell us that God created this world and it was perfect. It's not a matter of knowing how God created the universe and this world. What does matter is why God created this world and human beings. He created human beings to live with Him in His eternal Heavenly Kingdom, to enjoy His presence and blessings for evermore, not to live only for this life and material possessions.

"What good will it be for someone to gain the whole world, yet forfeit their soul? Or what can anyone give in exchange for their soul?" (Matthew 16:26). Jesus went on to say, "Then he said to them, 'Watch out! Be on your guard against all kinds of greed; life does not consist in an abundance of possessions'" (Luke 12:15).

Throughout time people have desperately looked for answers to why there is so much suffering and pain. There are true, realistic answers with clear reasons why God allows people to suffer. Many of the reasons for suffering have numerous facets that are worth considering theologically, philosophically, rationally, and experientially.

Complicated as it may be, I am confident there is solid ground for evidence that God permitted suffering and pain as a tool to accomplish His purposes and plans.

There will always be people who keep asking, How can a good, loving, and caring God think it's all right to allow a world filled with diseases, disasters, death, accidents, crimes, and wars?

These and questions like them have plagued humankind since the beginning. Some of them have either hindered belief in God or kept countless individuals from believing in God altogether.

25

No Simple Answers To Prove God's Existence

Questions of this nature do not have simple, clear, or concise answers. There are a multitude of concepts that need to be dealt with when it comes to asking the "Whys" of life. Concepts like: how life and humans began, the reasons there is so much suffering in this world, proofs for the existence of God and life after death.

I have endeavored to grapple with them throughout my life. I argue that neither science, archaeology, mathematics, nor any other field of academic study will ever come up with anything that can prove God does not exist. In all my study and research, I believe there is more proof that God exists than not.

Therefore, I do not believe anyone can realistically call themselves an atheist. I believe one would need to know everything about the whole universe to say definitely there is no God. Essentially they would have to be like God to claim that. I believe the closest one can come to being an atheist is an agnostic. An agnostic is an individual who doesn't believe yet because they haven't seen enough evidence to their liking. Agnostics say, "Maybe God exists, maybe a Divine Being doesn't. I have not seen enough evidence yet come to a conclusion."

In fact, the Bible teaches that all human beings have an inner conviction that screams out that our existence is more than an issue of chance or being a lucky monkey in the evolutionary chain. Yes, something sets us apart from the animal kingdom. Nothing other than God can explain the complexities of the human body, our longing for an afterlife, and our belief in the absolutes of right and wrong. Everything we see in this world is predicated on the overwhelming proofs that God exists and He created this universe.

"For since the creation of the world God's invisible qualities—his eternal power and divine nature—have been clearly seen, being understood from what has been made, so that people are without excuse" (Romans 1:2).

"The heavens declare the glory of God; the skies proclaim the work of his hands" (Psalm 19:1).

"Indeed, when Gentiles, who do not have the law, do by nature things required by the law, they are a law for themselves, even though they do not have the law" (Romans 2:14). I believe everyone has a God-given conscience.

James MacDonald, a pastor, radio Bible teacher, and author of a book titled *When Life is Hard,* puts it this way: "God promises that if you will ask for wisdom in *your trials* that He will give it to you. If you humble yourself before the Lord, and say, *'I want to know why You've allowed this trial. What are You trying to teach me, Lord, and where can I begin to work on myself first." (1)*

These are more the type of questions God will answer when you're struggling with the trials of suffering. He goes on to explain more about the differences between general and personal questions God will answer:

> God doesn't answer the "existential why" as in, "Why do bad things happen to good people?" I think there are some good answers to that question, but that's not what this is about.
>
> God doesn't answer the "ultimatum why" as in, "You had better tell me why this is happening right now, God." (Like you're going to intimidate Him?)
>
> God doesn't answer the "observation why," as in, "Why doesn't my neighbor have to go through this, God?"
>
> The "why" that God will answer is the "personal why" "Why did You allow this in me now, God? What do You want to teach me?" You get to Him with that. "If I remain under here, God, what are the things that You want to work on? What's next in

Your plan of transformation for me?" God
answers that "why" in a hurry. (2)

We may never know all the particulars to every "why"
for our suffering, but we can know the personal aspects
God is attempting to develop for our character and
spiritual growth. The goal is asking the right questions
of God when we suffer.

The correct questions should lead you to look at the
first chapters of Genesis and see that God did make
a perfect world, where there was no evil, pain, or
suffering. To check man's ability to choose to love and
obey God with his own mind and will, God tested Adam
and Eve to prove their allegiance. However, they failed
that test, and that's how sin, sickness, and suffering
entered this world.

God Sees the Bigger Picture

Theologian Norman Geisler and renowned author and
apologist Ravi Zacharias make a good statement about
this in their book, *Who Made God? And Answers to
Over 100 Other Tough Questions of Faith.*

> Sometimes we humans wonder why God
> allows us to go through certain painful
> circumstances. But just because we find
> it difficult to imagine what reasons God
> could have does not mean that no such

reason exists. From our finite human perspective, we are often only able to see a few threads of the great tapestry of life and of the will of God. We do not have the full picture. That is why God calls us to trust him (see Hebrews 11). God sees the full picture and does not make mistakes. He has a reason for allowing painful circumstances to come our way— even if we cannot grasp it.

Geisler gives us something important to think about in this regard: Even in our finiteness, it is possible for humans to discover some good purposes for pain— such as warning us of greater evil (an infant need only touch a hot stove once to learn not to do it again), and to keep us from self-destruction (our built-in nerve endings detect pain so we won't, for example, continue to hold a hot pan in our hands). If finite humans can discover some good purposes for evil, then surely an infinitely wise God has a good purpose for all suffering. We may not understand that purpose in the temporal "now," but it nonetheless exists. Our inability to discern why bad things sometimes happen to us does not disprove God's benevolence; it merely exposes our ignorance. (3)

All the questioning we have toward God must lead us to start at the beginning of the Bible, way back in the book of Genesis.

Suffering Brings Us Back to Genesis

The Bible tells us, "In the beginning God created" a perfect world where He did not allow suffering and pain. This naturally is the kind of world we all wanted. "God saw all that he had made, and it was very good" (Genesis 1:31).

God gave the human race the best kind of world we would ever have wanted. There was no sickness, pain, or death. Everything was perfect. We can only dream or wish that this is how it could have been throughout human history.

"The LORD God took the man and put him in the Garden of Eden to work it and take care of it. And the LORD God commanded the man, "You are free to eat from any tree in the garden; but you must not eat from the tree of the knowledge of good and evil, for when you eat from it you will certainly die" (Genesis 2:15-17).

According to the passage above, God had to give mankind free will so people could determine whether or not they would love and obey God on their own. There had to be a way man could be tested collectively

31

through Adam and Eve in the garden with the tree of the knowledge of good and evil.

The first human beings lived in a perfect world. All they had to do was stay away from the tree of forbidden fruit. But rebellion, pride, ego, and selfishness won out. Man failed God's test. The Scriptures allude to the truth that Adam and Eve represented every human being. We all would have failed the test because of our free will and sinful natures. "All have sinned and fallen short of the glory of God" (Romans 3:23).

There's a longer passage in the Bible that elaborates on this truth principle. It too is in the book of Genesis.

> Now the serpent was craftier than any of the wild animals the LORD God had made. He said to the woman, "Did God really say, 'You must not eat from any tree in the garden'?" The woman said to the serpent, "We may eat fruit from the trees in the garden, but God did say, 'You must not eat fruit from the tree that is in the middle of the garden, and you must not touch it, or you will die.'"
>
> "You will not certainly die," the serpent said to the woman. "For God knows that when you eat from it your eyes will be

opened and you will be like God, knowing good and evil."

When the woman saw that the fruit of the tree was good for food and pleasing to the eye, and also desirable for gaining wisdom, she took some and ate it. She also gave some to her husband, who was with her, and he ate it. Then the eyes of both of them were opened, and they realized they were naked; so they sewed fig leaves together and made coverings for themselves. (Genesis 3:1-7)

This act of disobedience brought mankind's alienation from God. It brought separation and pain. Some will ask, "Didn't God know this was going to happen?" And I must say, "Yes."

Then naturally the question comes back, "If God knew this was going to happen, didn't He set mankind up for failure?" I answer, "It may appear so, but God knew it was the only way to create creatures, made in His image, with free will and volition to choose or accept Him as the Creator."

Anyone who desires to be a parent has to realize that there are no guarantees your children will always love you. They will not always have a smooth and easy life. Some children may have to suffer serious illnesses either at birth, shortly thereafter, or later on in life. Others may experience a lot of suffering and even die young. Still other children can grow up to be criminals and even murder others.

Despite this parents decide to take the risk and have children. Fathers and mothers hope for the best that their children will live meaningful, long lives. They understand there are no guarantees that any of their children won't suffer or experience tragedies.

That's how God was. The triune God, the Father, the Son, and the Holy Spirit, though contented from all eternity to be with each other, were moved to create human beings in their image who could share in all the blessings and benefits heaven could offer. To God, the risks were worth it.

This Perfect World Became Broken and Cursed

The sin of man caused this world to become corrupted. Death and decay became the norm for this world. Adam and Eve were barred from the garden of Eden, and that perfect condition for the world ceased.

> To Adam he said, "Because you listened to your wife and ate fruit from the tree about which I commanded you, you must not eat from it, Cursed is the ground because of you; through painful toil you will eat

food from it all the days of your life. It will produce thorns and thistles for you and you will eat the plants of the field. By the sweat of your brow you will eat your food until you return to the ground, since from it you were taken; for dust you are and to dust you will return." (Genesis 3:17-19)

Here we see what happened to this perfect world. We see why everything was cursed because of the judgment for sin. God designed this world in such a way that He would use pain, problems, and people to accomplish His purpose in the lives of individuals by supplying them with strength and comfort through Bible promises.

We see this explained in the book of Romans:

I consider that our present sufferings are not worth comparing with the glory that will be revealed in us. For the creation waits in eager expectation for the children of God to be revealed. For the creation was subjected to frustration, not by its own choice, but by the will of the one who subjected it, in hope that the creation itself will be liberated from its bondage to decay and brought into the freedom and glory of the children of God.

> We know that the whole creation has been
> groaning as in the pains of childbirth right
> up to the present time. Not only so, but
> we ourselves, who have the first fruits
> of the Spirit, groan inwardly as we wait
> eagerly for our adoption to son-ship, the
> redemption of our bodies. For in this hope
> we were saved. But hope that is seen is
> no hope at all. Who hopes for what they
> already have? But if we hope for what we
> do not yet have, we wait for it patiently.
> (Romans 8:18-25)

This remarkable portion of Scripture tells us that suffering is a part of this world because of the curse of sin. The earth was subjected to the bondage of decay, disease, and death. The planet and we ourselves as human beings will age, wear out, and die. But for believers in Christ, whatever they go through in life will be a distant memory when they finally get to Heaven. There's so much more waiting for follower of God and the Bible in the afterlife. Whatever one has to endure on this earth will pale in comparison to what will be revealed to them in Heaven.

The world you are born into is not the final resting place. This place is corrupted because of the judgment given to it as a result of sin and disobedience. It does not matter how much glitter, electric lights, beautiful architecture, fine dining, music, or entertainment is shown in this world, because it is in bondage to decay and suffering. It is a dead end to live for and look to this world as the best place to make you happy.

Digging into the Scriptures, commentaries, and books will help you "establish a theology for suffering." Having a theology means you have discovered biblical answers, principles, and truths about how to build a strong foundation for your lives to stand on when suffering comes.

CHAPTER 3

Establishing a Theology About Suffering

A s doctors kept searching for answers to my medical emergency and various treatments to keep me on the way to recovery, I was reminded that spiritually, everyone should search for answers to their own sin dilemma.

The Bible teaches that mankind has a spiritual sickness that led to eternal death and separation from God. Symptoms of this malady are fear of God, anxiety about dying, wondering about life after death, a hole in the spiritual heart, emptiness from materialism, alienation from God, and others.

All of these spiritual symptoms must cause one to seek out the Great Physician, the only healer for the soul, the God of the Bible, both Old and New Testament, which reveals Jesus Christ. Searching the Scriptures about suffering will help one establish a firm foundational theology for pain and affliction.

The word *theology* is a combination of two Greek words: *theos,* meaning "God," and *apologia,* meaning "to make a defense" or "to develop a system for establishing beliefs." Together the words for *theology* mean "the study about God and the established system of beliefs called doctrines of the Bible."

These doctrines lead one to the unique study theologians call the Trinity. The word *Trinity* is not actually found in the Bible. However, the concept of what this word came to mean is deeply entwined in revealing God's being and character. The Scriptures often refer to a plurality of individuals making up one entity as in the case of the triune God. Notice the following verses when they speak of two becoming one:

"That is why a man leaves his father and mother and is united to his wife, and they become one flesh" (Genesis 2:24).

"For this reason a man will leave his father and mother and be united to his wife, and the two will become one flesh. This is a profound mystery—but I am talking about Christ and the church" (Ephesians 5:31-32).

Or do you not know that he who is joined to a harlot is one body *with her?* For "the two," He says, "shall become one flesh" (1 Corinthians 6:15-17).

"For as the body is one and has many members, but all the members of that one body, being many, are one body, so also *is* Christ" (1 Corinthians 12:11-13).

The Doctrine of the Trinity and Suffering

Man's fall into sin was no surprise to God. Since He is all-knowing, He realized when man sinned that there had to be a plan for redemption. God was not going to remain aloof or uninvolved. In fact the triune Godhead, made up of the Father, the Son, and the Holy Spirit, knew they would be actively involved in reaching out to the beings made in God's image.

Mysteriously, the God of the Bible has revealed Himself as one divine being consisting of three distinct persons. Not three gods, but one God in complete unity of three persons.

The truth of the Trinity can be complicated and the majority of biblical scholars throughout the church age have believed and taught it. But it too is a matter of faith and mystery regarding how the Godhead works together and has existed throughout eternity. Suffice it to say that for this topic on suffering, it must be dealt with as practically and simply as possible.

The doctrine of the Trinity helps explain how the Godhead could identify with mankind and provide the perfect sacrifice for the forgiveness necessary between God and man. God Himself could come to earth and bear all the suffering from the curse of sin to provide the way for human beings to enter the kingdom of God.

The second person of what we call the Trinity, Jesus Christ, would actually come to this earth and take on human flesh.

The Christian doctrine of the Trinity speaks volumes on how He could have allowed suffering to enter the world. God knew all along that a person in the Godhead would come to take on human flesh and be offered up as the perfect sacrifice for sin.

Every sacrifice for sin in the Jewish religion as told in the Old Testament looked forward to the messianic sacrificial Lamb. The New Testament looked back to the sacrificial Lamb on the cross in Jesus Christ.

Eventually, with God's redemption plan, there would rise up a people He would call His own who would worship Him as a benevolent, loving, compassionate God. Don't forget that God is not aloof from the fact that His redemption plan was going to cause Him to take on human flesh and come to the earth He created to be rejected, ridiculed, and reviled by the beings He made "in His image."

Revelation 13:8 says, "The Lamb slain from the foundation of the world." This refers to the truth that God knew Christ, the sacrificial Lamb, was going to be crucified before He created the world of men and women.

There are many allusions to the plurality of the Godhead when we see Scriptures that refer to God as "us."

"Then God said, 'Let us make man (humankind) in our image, after our likeness." Notice God did not say, "Let us make man in my image." Doesn't it sound strange to say *us* and *our*? God was not referring to angels or other beings as *us* or *our*. He was referring to Himself as a plurality (Genesis 1:26). In Genesis regarding the Tower of Babel, God said, "Come let us go down and there confuse their language, so that they may not understand one another's speech" (Genesis 11:7 [ESV]).

As I said, many theologians and Bible scholars believe the Bible clearly portrays a God who has a plural nature, one God in three persons with total unity and purpose. There is no jealousy or competition. It is referred to as a plural Godhead. Remember Jesus said of marriage partners, "The two will become one" (Matthew 19:5). A triune God is very practical and clearly alluded to in Scripture. (See Genesis 1:26, 3:22; Isaiah 6:3, 8, 11:2-3, 42:1, 48:16; Matthew 3:16-17, 28:19.)

In the second person of the Trinity, Jesus Christ, as God, would be able to suffer crucifixion on a cross to serve as the ultimate sacrificial atonement for the sins of the world. God's brilliant manifestation of Him being one God, made up of three persons—in the Father, Son, and Holy Spirit, what theologically is termed the

Holy Trinity—gives Jehovah God the ability to allow the second person of the Trinity, Jesus Christ, as Deity, to take on human flesh and experience the miraculous virgin birth through Mary. Christ became the messianic, sacrificial Lamb whom Judaism and its prophets of Scripture foretold and were looking for.

"The Word became flesh and made his dwelling among us. We have seen his glory, the glory of the one and only Son, who came from the Father, full of grace and truth" (John 1:14).

The late Dr. Stanley Horton, one of my seminary professors, said, "A vivid (example of the Trinity) is given in the events clearly surrounding the baptism of Jesus at the Jordan River by John the Baptist: "As soon as Jesus was baptized, he went up out of the water. At that moment heaven was opened, and he saw the Spirit of God descending like a dove and alighting on him. And a voice from heaven said, 'This is my Son, whom I love; with him I am well pleased'" (Matthew 3:16-17). (1)

The whole Godhead was represented as the Father spoke from heaven, the Son was in the water and the Spirit descended upon Him.

Jesus said, "Therefore go and make disciples of all nations, baptizing them in the name of the Father and of the Son and of the Holy Spirit" (Matthew 28:19) and again here, "John saw Jesus coming toward him and said, "Look, the Lamb of God, who takes away the sin of the world!" (John 1:29).

Jesus Was the True Suffering Servant

New Testament scholars believe Jesus was a fulfillment of biblical prophesies concerning the coming of the Messiah. Christ was called the suffering servant in the Old Testament book of Isaiah.

> He grew up before him like a tender shoot, and like a root out of dry ground. He had no beauty or majesty to attract us to him, nothing in his appearance that we should desire him. He was despised and rejected by mankind, a man of suffering, and familiar with pain. Like one from whom people hide their faces he was despised, and we held him in low esteem.
>
> Surely he took up our pain and bore our suffering, yet we considered him punished by God, stricken by him, and afflicted. But he was pierced for our transgressions, he was crushed for our iniquities; the punishment that brought us peace was on him, and by his wounds we are healed. We all, like sheep, have gone astray, each of us has turned to our own way; and the

Lᴏʀᴅ has laid on him the iniquity of us all.
(Isaiah 53:2-6)

The writers of the New Testament clearly saw these passages in Isaiah as referring to Jesus Christ.

The book of Acts records an instance when a devout Ethiopian eunuch had a scroll of Isaiah.

> On his way he (Philip) met an Ethiopian eunuch, an important official in charge of all the treasury of the Kandake (which means "queen of the Ethiopians"). This man had gone to Jerusalem to worship, and on his way home was sitting in his chariot reading the Book of Isaiah the prophet. The Spirit told Philip, "Go to that chariot and stay near it."
>
> Then Philip ran up to the chariot and heard the man reading Isaiah the prophet. "Do you understand what you are reading?" Philip asked.
>
> "How can I," he said, "unless someone explains it to me?" So he invited Philip to come up and sit with him."
>
> This is the passage of Scripture the eunuch was reading: "He was led like a

sheep to the slaughter, and as a lamb
before its shearer is silent, so he did not
open his mouth. In his humiliation he was
deprived of justice. Who can speak of his
descendants? For his life was taken from
the earth."

The eunuch asked Philip, "Tell me, please,
who is the prophet talking about, himself
or someone else?" Then Philip began with
that very passage of Scripture and told
him the good news about Jesus.

As they traveled along the road, they
came to some water and the eunuch said,
"Look, here is water. What can stand in
the way of my being baptized?" And he
gave orders to stop the chariot. Then both
Philip and the eunuch went down into the
water and Philip baptized him. When they
came up out of the water, the Spirit of the
Lord suddenly took Philip away, and the
eunuch did not see him again, but went
on his way rejoicing. (Acts 8:27-39)

The apostle Peter even quoted this Isaiah passage in
his first epistle:

For it is commendable if someone bears up
under the pain of unjust suffering because

they are conscious of God … But if you suffer for doing good and you endure it, this is commendable before God. To this you were called, because Christ suffered for you, leaving you an example that you should follow in his steps. He committed no sin, and no deceit was found in his mouth.

When they hurled their insults at him, he did not retaliate; when he suffered, he made no threats. Instead, he entrusted himself to him who judges justly. 'He himself bore our sins' in his body on the cross, so that we might die to sins and live for righteousness; 'by his wounds you have been healed.' For 'you were like sheep going astray,' but now you have returned to the Shepherd and Overseer of your souls. (1 Peter 2:19-25)

Jesus was our supreme example of suffering. His whole life was marked by suffering. He suffered the emotional pain of His own family and people rejecting Him. He was cursed at, laughed at, despised, and rejected. He suffered the most excruciating physical pain of His day. It was called crucifixion.

We can see Jesus' own humanity when He cried out during the pinnacle of His pain, suffering, and isolation from the Heavenly Father: "About three in the afternoon Jesus cried out in a loud voice, '*Eli, Eli, lema sabachthani?*' (which means 'My God, my God, why have you forsaken me?')" (Matthew 27:46).

This verse was a prophetic quote Jesus used from Psalm 27:1 to express His ultimate loneliness. For the first time in all eternity, God the Father had to turn away from Him because all the sins of mankind were placed on Him to bear and to provide atonement for.

What love Jesus exhibited here as He totally identified with every human being who ever cried out in the depths of their pain the inevitable "Why." Jesus Himself said, "Why have you forsaken me, Father God? Where are you?" Jesus revealed here that He felt what it was like to be totally human and facing incredible pain and isolation from God.

In Christ we have a definite high priest who can identify with how we feel and offer up intercession on our behalf to the Heavenly Father:

"For we do not have a high priest who is unable to empathize with our weaknesses, but we have one who has been tempted in every way, just as we are—yet he did not sin. Let us then approach God's throne of grace with confidence, so that we may receive mercy and find grace to help us in our time of need" (Hebrews 4:15-16).

Jesus was beaten, whipped, pushed, shoved, made to carry a heavy wooden beam, and crowned with thorns jammed into his skull. Isaiah records, "Just as there were many who were appalled at him his appearance was so disfigured beyond that of any human being and his form marred beyond human likeness" (Isaiah 52:14).

This passage tells us Jesus was beaten beyond human recognition. Imagine what Jesus' face could have looked like if the crucifiers had grabbed pieces of His beard and ripped it off His face. Jesus came to earth with the express purpose of suffering. He was acquainted with grief and suffering.

Not only does Jesus embody suffering, but He clearly shows us God Himself was not immune to the suffering that resulted from man's sin. God, who allowed suffering for a reason, epitomized what suffering was meant to accomplish through His own life. God's ultimate suffering was the means that would allow a time where there would be no more suffering forever.

Christ's Afflictions and the Church

"Now I rejoice in what I am suffering for you, and I fill up in my flesh what is still lacking in regard to Christ's afflictions, for the sake of his body, which is the church" (Colossians 1:24).

Paul was saying that he could rejoice, knowing that he was being an example of enduring suffering and afflictions in the same way Christ did. Others who knew Paul and could see him probably never saw Christ's suffering personally.

Therefore people could see Paul in his time, which could make up for the fact that they didn't actually see Jesus' afflictions firsthand. What was referred to as lacking, in the verse above, was that people who could not see Christ's sufferings personally could see Paul's suffering and that of any other future believers who would suffer afflictions for the sake of following in Christ's steps.

All this was done to spread the gospel message for the church, the body of Christ. Christ was the supreme example of suffering afflictions in many ways.

Jesus left His followers with an example of how they could bear up under suffering various kinds of afflictions. God has called many Christians throughout the ages as people like Paul, who are examples of suffering for the cause of Christ to the people of their day. Today, it could be you.

Suffering and Free Will

However, the question that still presents itself is why would God create beings with a free will so that they would choose to disobey and experience untold suffering and evil? We find the answer in the book of Genesis, which records the beginnings of the parameters God set up for humankind to follow, thus testing their free will. The Garden of Eden had the Tree of Life in it as the test for the beings God created to obey. They were told not to eat the fruit on the Tree of the Knowledge of Good and Evil.

This world was perfect, with no death, evil, tragedy, pain, or suffering. But God knew the dreaded truth that man would sin even if the cost and punishment was going to be horrendous and gut wrenching.

G. K. Chesterton, a well-known Christian apologist of the early 1900s, in his work titled *Orthodoxy,* said, "According to most philosophers, God in making the world enslaved it. According to Christianity, in making it, He set it free. God had written, not so much a poem, but rather a play; a play he had planned as perfect, but which had necessarily been left to human actors and stage-managers, who had since made a great mess of it." (2)

Genesis 3 records the judgment that was death, both spiritual and physical, as banishment from God's presence; it was a broken world of death, decay, pain, suffering, and evil. Mankind has struggled to grapple with these issues ever since. It has served as a roadblock to faith and belief in accepting God's goodness, grace, and compassion.

The world became a place of evil, murder, war, accidents, and tragedies. There have been untold numbers of inhumane actions that human beings have afflicted upon each other, from the audacities of tortures and imprisonments, to the creation of devices and weapons of mass destruction.

C. S. Lewis, a famous apologist and prolific writer for the Christian faith, wrote this about free will:

> God created things which had free will. That means creatures which can go wrong or right. Some people think they can imagine a creature which was free but had no possibility of going wrong, but I can't. If a thing is free to be good it's also free to be bad. And free will is what has made evil possible. Why, then, did God give them free will? Because free will, though it makes evil possible, is also the only thing that makes possible any love or goodness or joy worth having ... God knew what would happen if they used their freedom the wrong way: apparently, He thought it worth the risk. If God thinks this state of war in the universe a price worth paying for free will-that is, for

> making a real world in which creatures
> can do real good or harm and something
> of real importance can happen, instead
> of a toy world which only moves when
> He pulls the strings-then we may take it
> is worth paying. (3)

History is replete with the terrible evils that human beings have done to each other, and this broken planet has erupted with such natural catastrophes as earthquakes, hurricanes, tsunamis, tornados, floods, and fires. Still God is revealed in the Bible as a benevolent being of grace, redemption, forgiveness, and compassion. How can all this be reconciled?

To properly grasp all the reasons God had for allowing suffering and evil to be a part of this earth, one must understand that God has many mysteries surrounding His ways that finite human beings cannot understand with their limited reasoning.

A Divine Mystery Between Faith and Free Will

In principle God gave human beings a free will so they could cooperate with Him and obey His commands. Yet they still need His assistance to truly come to a place where they believe in His existence. In all reality you really cannot argue someone into belief in God and the validity of the Bible; it's a matter of the heart and faith.

There is no way to prove there is a God in a scientific lab or test tube. No one can make God speak to them audibly in a loud voice from the sky as the apostle Paul did (Acts 8); nor can anyone cause God to perform a miracle any time they want one to prove He exists.

Atheist philosopher David Hume said, "The Christian religion not only was at first attended with miracles, but even at this day cannot be believed by any reasonable person without one." (4)

There are many skeptics and unbelievers who insist that scientific or pragmatic reasoning will not allow one to believe in the existence of God or an afterlife. They say supernatural miracles do not exist.

A mystery exists when it comes to faith for a conversion to Christ. There are reasonable arguments one can use to defend their Christian faith. Some of them are the accuracy of the New Testament documents, archaeological discoveries, proofs for the resurrection of Christ and the believers whose lives have been changed throughout Church history.

It is illustrated in the Gospel of Luke shortly after Christ rose from the dead. A couple of disciples were leaving Jerusalem on the road to Emmaus. They were in shock from Jesus' crucifixion and death. Unknown to them the Lord made a post-resurrection appearance, but their physical eyes and spiritual eyes were closed to seeing that it was Christ in His resurrected body.

The following passage is from Luke 24:13-35:

> Now, that same day two of them were going to a village called Emmaus, about seven miles from Jerusalem. They were talking with each other about everything that had happened. As they talked and discussed these things with each other, Jesus himself came up and walked along with them; but they were kept from recognizing him.
>
> He asked them, "What are you discussing together as you walk along?" They stood still, their faces downcast. One of them, named Cleopas, asked him, "Are you the only one visiting Jerusalem who does not know the things that have happened there in these days?"
>
> "What things?" he asked. "About Jesus of Nazareth," they replied. "He was a prophet, powerful in word and deed before God and all the people. The chief priests and our rulers handed him over to be sentenced to death, and they crucified him; but we had hoped that he was the

one who was going to redeem Israel. And what is more, it is the third day since all this took place. In addition, some of our women amazed us. They went to the tomb early this morning but didn't find his body. They came and told us that they had seen a vision of angels, who said he was alive. Then some of our companions went to the tomb and found it just as the women had said, but they did not see Jesus."

He said to them, "How foolish you are, and how slow to believe all that the prophets have spoken! Did not the Messiah have to suffer these things and then enter his glory?" And beginning with Moses and all the Prophets, he explained to them what was said in all the Scriptures concerning himself."

As they approached the village to which they were going, Jesus continued on as if he were going farther. But they urged him strongly, "Stay with us, for it is nearly evening; the day is almost over." So he went in to stay with them.

When he was at the table with them, he took bread, gave thanks, broke it and

began to give it to them. Then their eyes
were opened and they recognized him,
and he disappeared from their sight. They
asked each other "Were not our hearts
burning within us while he talked with us
on the road and opened the Scriptures
to us?"

They got up and returned at once to
Jerusalem. There they found the Eleven
and those with them, assembled together
and saying, "It is true! The Lord has risen
and has appeared to Simon." Then the
two told what had happened on the way,
and how Jesus was recognized by them
when he broke the bread.

We clearly see, in this passage, how humans can be
spiritually blind and unable to see the truth about God
and His existence. Then all of a sudden something
miraculously changes and belief occurs. It's as if
spiritually blind eyes were opened.

How Free Will and Faith Work Together

Numerous Scriptures attest to the divine mystery of
how individuals arrive at a personal faith in the great
God and Savior, Jesus Christ. I believe we get a clue
for this answer from a verse in Revelation 3:20, which
says, "Here I am! I stand at the door and knock. If

anyone hears my voice and opens the door, I will come in and eat with that person, and they with me."

When God knocks on the door of your heart, which means your soul, mind, will, thoughts, and emotions, it's important to listen. He may knock through a myriad of things such as a trial, tragedy, illness, accident, something you read, a sermon you may have heard, a conversation with someone, and so on. Then strangely you open the door of your heart, and this is where free will comes in. You cry out, silently or aloud, "God, help me. God, I need you. Lord, I want to believe in you. Jesus, if you're there, come into my life and forgive me of my sins."

All of a sudden you believe, you are inexplicably enlightened, and you can see how the Bible and God all make sense. It gives you peace and assurance about the meaning of life. You realize that God truly did create this universe, that something can't appear out of nothing, that absolutes do exist from an almighty God. This is the essence where fact and faith merge together; hopeless unbelief is replaced by hope-filled faith.

God told the apostle Paul, "I will rescue you from your own people and from the Gentiles. I am sending you to them to open their eyes and turn them from darkness to light and from the power of Satan to God, so that they may receive forgiveness of sins and a place among those who are sanctified by faith in me" (Acts 26:17-18).

God spoke about how sin and doubt will prevent one from coming to faith. "For this people's heart has become calloused; they hardly hear with their ears, and they have closed their eyes. Otherwise they might see with their eyes, hear with their ears, understand with their hearts and turn, and I would heal them" (Acts 28:27).

Jesus referred to this when He said, "No one can come to me unless the Father who sent me draws them, and I will raise them up at the last day" (John 6:44).

We see this mystery of faith when a woman was listening to Paul speak about Christ, and it was the opportunity for her to respond to God knocking on the door of her heart. She responded by faith. "One of those listening was a woman from the city of Thyatira named Lydia, a dealer in purple cloth. She was a worshiper of God. The Lord opened her heart to respond to Paul's message" (Acts 16:14).

This truth is further seen here: "Consequently, faith comes from hearing the message, and the message is heard through the word about Christ" (Romans 10:17).

In the midst of a suffering, fallen and broken world the God of all comfort can appear and people can hear the gospel message knocking at their heart. The Lord can open their heart, and then they decide with their mind and make the decision to believe in and surrender to Christ, thus receiving meaning, hope, eternal life, and faith.

God Will Do What Is Right

Ultimately the Jehovah God of the Old and New Testament deserves to be trusted, that His plans and purposes have an ultimate, eternally beneficial outcome for many lives. God alone, as the most righteous judge, will do what is right regarding His creation and created human beings.

Those who believe in His redemptive plan of life and forgiveness will receive eternal life. Those who chose not to believe and follow His ways will be judged according to His standards of justice and judgment.

The New Testament book of Romans tells us God has His own plan to deal with those who have never heard about His redemption and salvation. We must leave that in His hands.

> All who sin apart from the law will also perish apart from the law, and all who sin under the law will be judged by the law.

For it is not those who hear the law who are righteous in God's sight, but it is those who obey the law who will be declared righteous. (Indeed, when Gentiles, who do not have the law, do by nature things required by the law, they are a law for themselves, even though they do not have the law. They show that the requirements of the law are written on their hearts, their consciences also bearing witness, and their thoughts sometimes accusing them and at other times even defending them.) This will take place on the day when God judges people's secrets through Jesus Christ, as my gospel declares. (Romans 2:12-16)

When you hear the gospel of Jesus Christ, it reveals that you are sinful and need to repent and receive Christ's forgiveness. When that occurs, if you respond, God will grant the grace, openness, and strength to help you obey and follow the commands of His Word.

"If we claim to be without sin, we deceive ourselves and the truth is not in us. If we confess our sins, he is faithful and just and will forgive us our sins and purify us from all unrighteousness. If we claim we have not sinned, we make him out to be a liar and his word is not in us" (1 John 1:8-10).

"But what does it say? 'The word is near you; it is in your mouth and in your heart,' 'that is, the message concerning faith that we proclaim: If you declare with your mouth, 'Jesus is Lord,' and believe in your heart that God raised him from the dead, you will be saved" (Romans 10:8-10).

We are told that God will judge people living in a country or area, who have never heard the truths of the Gospel of Jesus Christ, in a special way. It will be according to how they've conducted themselves and followed "the requirements of God's laws that have been written on their hearts and consciences." God will rightly judge those who never heard the gospel ("good news") of Jesus Christ as they have lived according to their heart and conscience.

"How, then, can they call on the one they have not believed in? And how can they believe in the one of whom they have not heard? And how can they hear without someone preaching to them? And how can anyone preach unless they are sent? As it is written, 'How beautiful are the feet of those who bring good news!'" (Romans 10:14-15).

The key is not to allow questioning God's love about what happens to those who've never heard the gospel of Jesus Christ, to keep you from believing in Him when it's presented to you. One must concentrate on making a decision to believe in Christ if you have already heard the gospel and haven't yet believed and received Christ as Savior and Lord. The Bible says, "From everyone who has been given much, much will be demanded; and from the one who has been entrusted with much, much more will be asked" (Luke 12:48).

God's Presence in the Midst of Suffering

While in the hospital, I was blessed to be able to sense God's presence and strength, which gave me peace and comfort. In the long run God kept speaking to my inner heart through that still small inner voice. We see this phrase when God spoke to Elijah during his depression and discouragement: "And after the earthquake a fire, *but* the LORD *was* not in the fire; and after the fire a still small voice" (1 Kings 19:12).

If you'll listen to that inner voice in your heart, I believe you can hear God speaking to you that there is "value in suffering." Suffering is intended to be one of God's greatest tools to direct one's attention toward Him and what He says in the Bible.

CHAPTER 4

The Value of Suffering

This particular illness that put me at death's door reminded me that you never know when an emergency can hit you. I've always heard a shocking statement that says, "You should live your life as if any day could be your last." One can shake that off and ignore it, yet how true it is. It's not a bad idea to keep that thought in your mind from time to time.

I never planned or imagined I'd be sick enough to require hospitalization in an intensive care unit for a number of days. Yet here I was, God totally helping me survive my twelfth day in the hospital after the physical emergency.

One thing a follower of Christ can count on is receiving God's comfort and strength to help them bear up under suffering. God established the value of suffering as the greatest tool for Him to use in preparing His children to be conformed to His image. In the same way parents discipline children with love and not anger to help them learn the blessings of obedience. God uses suffering as discipline to teach His children many lessons. I can hear our Heavenly Father saying what most parents do: "This hurts me more than it does you."

You find New Testament writings of the apostle Paul that address this truth. Here are a few of them he shared in his letters to various churches throughout Asia Minor, Greece, and Italy in the cities of Rome, Corinth, Philippi, and Thessalonica:

"We also glory in our sufferings, because we know that suffering produces perseverance" (Romans 5:3). "Now if we are children, then we are heirs—heirs of God and co-heirs with Christ, if indeed we share in his sufferings in order that we may also share in his glory. I consider that our present sufferings are not worth comparing with the glory that will be revealed in us" (Romans 8:17-18).

"Just as we share abundantly in the sufferings of Christ, so also our comfort abounds through Christ. If we are distressed, it is for your comfort and salvation; if we are comforted, it is for your comfort, which produces in you patient endurance of the same sufferings we suffer. And our hope for you is firm, because we know that just as you share in our sufferings, so also you share in our comfort." (2 Corinthians 1:5-7)

Paul said this to the believers in Philippi and Thessalonica: "I want to know Christ—yes, to know the power of his resurrection and participation in his sufferings, becoming like him in his death" (Philippians 3:10). "You became imitators of us and of the Lord, for you welcomed the message in the midst of severe suffering with the joy given by the Holy Spirit" (1 Thessalonians 1:6). "All this is evidence that God's judgment is right, and as a result you will be counted worthy of the kingdom of God, for which you are suffering" (2 Thessalonians 1:5).

To his beloved young friend and colleague Timothy he said, "So do not be ashamed of the testimony about our Lord or of me his prisoner. Rather, join with me in suffering for the gospel, by the power of God" (1 Timothy 1:8).

No More Than You Can Handle

I know that many of these verses can sound high, lofty, and unattainable. But numerous individuals and families going through suffering and hard times have received spiritual and practical benefit from them.

When someone has to go through trials or suffering, you often hear a well-meaning person say, "God will never give you more than you can handle." Every so often that phrase would bother me. I sometimes felt like saying something to God like, "You've got to be kidding me. Are you sure? I can't take it anymore. God, you certainly mustn't really know me. Otherwise you wouldn't allow this to be happening."

What does that phrase mean anyway? I believe it came from 1 Corinthians 10:13, which says, "No temptation has overtaken you except what is common to mankind. And God is faithful; he will not let you be tempted beyond what you can bear. But when you are tempted, he will also provide a way out so that you can endure it."

The translation of the Bible called *The Message* puts it this way: "No test or temptation that comes your way is beyond the course of what others have had to face. All you need to remember is that God will never let you down; he'll never let you be pushed past your limit; he'll always be there to help you come through it."

The original Greek word used in the New Testament for the word *suffering* is also used for *passion,* transliterated as *"pathema,"* which means "that which one suffers or has suffered externally, a suffering, misfortune, calamity, (passions of sin) and evil, and affliction of the sufferings of Christ. It speaks of the afflictions which Christians must undergo in behalf of the same cause which Christ patiently endured of an inward state, an affliction, undergoing the passion of enduring a suffering." (See Romans 7:5, 8:18; 2 Corinthians 1:5-7; 2 Timothy 3:11.) (1)

Another Greek word, transliterated as *"peirasmos,"* means "temptations and trials," and is used often in the New Testament. It refers to "a mental state, by which we are enticed to sin." It can also refer to "adversity, affliction or trouble sent by God serving to

test or prove one's character, faith or holiness." (See
1 Corinthians 10:13.) (2)

I believe this Scripture is addressing those who are
His committed followers and disciples and saying
that God will not allow any suffering, test, trial, or
temptation to come their way to destroy them. He
reminds them that they are not alone in what they are
going through. Other children of God have experienced
similar sufferings too.

Though it is often questioned, I had to learn to accept
that "God will not give you more than you can bear."
He will not let you be "pushed beyond your limitations."
The Lord explains that if you hang in there and don't
give up, He'll provide a way of escape or be there
to help you get through it. He knows that we, in our
humanness, are really unable to bear much on our own
without His help.

In this verse we see a promise that says God is faithful
and won't give us more than we can handle. He will
make a way of escape that will allow us to be able to
bear it.

Here are some of those major escapes: prayer,
promises from the Bible, the power and strength of
the Holy Spirit, fellow Christians standing alongside
you to provide encouragement, meditation on the Bible
and good Christian literature, listening to gospel music

and worship choruses, and hearing good sermons and teachings from God's Word.

These and many other steps are given by God to provide various ways of escape so you can bear the suffering, testing, and trials.

Whether occasionally or often, you may feel as if you can't handle suffering or take it anymore. It no doubt takes faith, hope, and trust in God to endure difficulties and suffering.

Yet there is an element of what I call "the mystical"—a place where you must rely on God's Holy Spirit to empower your spiritual nature to accept what you cannot feel or see. It's getting to the place of inevitable faith that says, "I'm going to love and trust God through it all, no matter what." It's the kind of faith talked about in the New Testament book of Hebrews, chapter 11: "Now faith is confidence in what we hope for and assurance about what we do not see" (Hebrews 11:1).

The Message puts it this way: "The fundamental fact of existence is that this trust in God, this faith, is the firm foundation under everything that makes life worth living. It's our handle on what we can't see. The act of faith is what distinguished our ancestors, set them above the crowd."

God Behind the Scenes

The remainder of Hebrews 11 records how many of the Jewish leaders and believers showed their faith in God to accomplish much and beat all odds by clinging to their belief in the God of Abraham, Isaac, and Jacob.

I know firsthand that when you are going through suffering and tough times, it is difficult to have faith in God. The Lord understands our frailties and weaknesses. Mercifully, God is with us whether or not we feel Him or see His hand in what we're going through. Even if we earnestly pray for Him to remove our pain, hurt, or grief and He does not and we feel like giving up, He'll stand by our side.

He tells us to trust that He's there working behind the scenes and accomplishing His divine will and purpose for our lives. Psalm 30:5 tells us, "Weeping may endure for the night but joy comes in the morning." No suffering for a child of God will last forever. There will be a time of eternal joy in the presence of the Lord.

After my personal experience of being at the doors of heaven, where I literally had a potential time of hours, minutes, or seconds before entering into eternity, God in His infinite mercy and grace kept me alive and on this earth.

He obviously had more He wanted to teach me about and continue to share with others. As someone said to me, "God had more work for you to do. He wasn't done with using you for His work on earth yet." Thus I'm still here for a reason. So however long I have on this earth, I desire with all my heart to live for Jesus Christ and give Him glory.

This World Gives Glimpses of God's Goodness

Regardless of how long suffering may last, realize that in this life of pain, God gives us glimpses of heaven's beauty, wonder, and awesomeness in this life. On one hand, suffering and pain play a big part in life through sadness, difficulties, sicknesses, and disappointments that come to every human being. On the other hand, God reveals just enough good and uplifting experiences to manifest the power of faith and the innate ability of human beings to endure obstacles and survive all odds.

Christian philosopher Blaise Pascal said, "In faith there is enough light for those who want to believe and enough shadow for those who don't." (3)

Let me put it another way: There's enough good in this world to reveal a good God as the Creator, and enough bad to show how this world is filled with so much selfishness, suffering, and evil, it could cause one to find it hard to believe in God.

You can see the goodness of God when you look at newborn babies, the love between family and friends, and the kind things people do for each other. God's creativity is also seen through paintings, music, sunrises, sunsets, oceans, beaches, mountains, stars, planets, and much, much more. On the other hand you can question God's existence and goodness when you see such chaos, catastrophes, and crimes.

God created this world with human beings so they could share all the beautiful blessings of this world. But after the curse of sin, this world became a fallen place and the blessings of God's goodness became harder to see and a matter of faith.

Therefore Heaven will reveal all the goodness and beauty God originally created men and women to enjoy in the Garden of Eden. In Heaven there is eternal joy and beauty beyond our wildest imagination. God shows small glimpses of it on this broken planet to cause His created beings to long for more than what this world offers.

Being Right with God Doesn't Make Life Easier

Some believe if you serve God, it will make your life easier and with enough faith you'll experience fewer problems. Sadly this ends up being a faulty way of thinking. Usually these people become disappointed and disillusioned leaving their faith in God devastated or weakened. This line of belief reveals they were serving God not for who He is but for what He may do.

They give you the feeling that if things had gone well for them or their family and friends, they'd believe in God. But if things didn't go well or work out positively, they say, "If there's a God, how could He have allowed this to happen? Therefore don't talk to me about having faith in God. I tried that and it doesn't work. There is no God."

It is wrong to compare and reduce God to someone like Santa Claus, a leprechaun or a good luck charm. God, who has revealed Himself in the Bible, has given enough reasons why anyone should have total faith and confidence in all the blessings of serving Him.

God does not exist only to provide for our comforts or for us to have a life of ease and prosperity. In fact biblically, the truth is that we are to exist for God, not that God exists only for us.

No Easy Life Promised

God doesn't promise an easy life. The Lord does not exist to give us a pain-free, smooth life. God has different purposes for each of His children and He specifically plots out their lives. Some may have it easier than others for reasons we'll never know in this life.

Very few biblical characters had an easy life. The person God chose to write almost two-thirds of the New Testament, the apostle Paul, was no stranger to suffering.

> Therefore, in order to keep me from becoming conceited, I was given a thorn in my flesh, a messenger of Satan, to torment me. Three times I pleaded with the Lord to take it away from me. But he said to me, "My grace is sufficient for you, for my power is made perfect in weakness." Therefore I will boast all the more gladly about my weaknesses, so that Christ's power may rest on me. That is why, for Christ's sake, I delight in weaknesses, in insults, in hardships, in persecutions, in difficulties. For when I am weak, then I am strong. (2 Corinthians 12:7-10)

The apostle Paul learned from experience through his relationship with Christ that God effectively uses and allows suffering to mold us and conform us into His image while developing our Christian character. Whether the suffering is physical, emotional, or spiritual, God uses all suffering for His glory to accomplish His divine purpose and will. The suffering can be temporary, occasional, long lasting, or chronic, yet any kind can be effective.

Some more benefits that contribute to the value of how God uses suffering are to get our attention, to keep us humble and dependent upon Him, and to allow His strength to show itself more powerfully as it flows out of our weaknesses, hardships, and difficulties. God's power is definitely "made perfect in weakness."

This line of thinking could lead someone to say, "If this is how it is then, why not delight in these tough and challenging circumstances and be open to more of them? Why pray for healing, or deliverance, or for God to remove it?" These are good questions.

However, it is not wrong to pray or ask others to pray for God's power to heal, or for a doctor to perform surgery or prescribe medicine, or for suffering to be shortened. God knows we are human. It's part of our nature to do all that's possible to alleviate pain and suffering. A great part of the Bible reveals the numerous times when God performed miracles of healing and deliverance from suffering.

On the other hand, we see just as many extended times where there is no miracle or deliverance from suffering. It's during those times when God works out His greater purposes for suffering.

In fact the apostle Paul said this very thing in the last Scripture quoted: "That is why, for Christ's sake, I delight in weaknesses." He was not being a pessimist or hopeless individual who didn't care. He was acting as one who wisely understood what God can and does accomplish through suffering and difficulties for "His glory." Paul truly believed that the sufferings that would not go away, receive God's miraculous healings, or be diminished or shortened were used for God's glory and purpose.

Surrender Your Burdens and Sufferings to Christ

Jesus reminds us to come to Him and surrender our burdens at His feet: "Come to me, all you who are weary and burdened, and I will give you rest. Take my yoke upon you and learn from me, for I am gentle and humble in heart, and you will find rest for your souls. For my yoke is easy and my burden is light" (Matthew 11:28-30).

Two oxen would be linked together in a harness so hard ground could be plowed or heavy things could be moved. Usually one smaller, younger, weaker ox would be teamed up with a stronger, older, more experienced ox that could bear more of the load. Jesus was telling us to link up with Him in His yoke or harness. In our weakness we could get into the yoke and team up with Him. His strength could pull us through the hard and tough times.

I can relate to this passage as I've often come to the Lord for strength and power to stay strong in the midst of suffering and pain. The Lord has helped me dedicate myself to the work of the ministry and all the duties it has entailed. Sometimes in my weakest moments God has come through to accomplish His greatest work.

Symbolisms in Life Relating to Suffering

Going through suffering in life can be symbolic of a mother struggling with all the discomforts and challenges of nine months of pregnancy. The actual delivery and birthing process culminates in unbelievable and excruciating pain. Yet all this becomes a distant memory after the infant is born, the umbilical cord is cut, and the baby is handed to the mother for that one-of-a-kind bonding process.

The believer will pass from this life of suffering to the glories of Heaven. Passing from Earth to Heaven can be compared to an unborn child leaving the womb to enter this great big world.

Another comparison is that of the caterpillar in the cocoon just before its transformation into a butterfly. A follower of Christ in this world of suffering is like a caterpillar that crawls slowly along. Only when it emerges from its cocoon does it become a beautiful butterfly, symbolic of the believer in Heaven.

It is also symbolic of a long, long trip on a passenger airliner. The plane gets you to your destination, but it often has cramped quarters and uncomfortable seats. The food's not the greatest, there's no place to stretch or move around, you have to breathe stale air, the restrooms are small, and there's no place to exercise or shower.

As a whole, when the flights lands, no one says, "Shucks, I don't want to get off the plane. I want to stay here longer." No, everyone can hardly wait to get off the plane. That's how it can and should be for a believer when the flight of their life's journey is over, when God says, "Come home, my child." Could it be that the believer, who suffered much and experienced a tough life of tribulations and trials, can be excited to get off the flight of life and enter their eternal reward and destination?

I was resolved and surrendered, ready to go to the place where, as Revelation 21:4 says, "There will be no more death or mourning or crying or pain, for the old order of things have passed away."

I was ready to get off the flight. I had been ready to accept God's will, whatever it was, for many, many years. Whether He wanted to keep me alive on this earth to accomplish more work for Him or was ready to take me home to Heaven, I often prayed, "Lord, Your will be done."

Suffering Is a Reminder That We're Living on Borrowed Time

This reminds me of a story about an American Airlines pilot on September 11, 2001 who experienced God's mysterious ways.

On September 10, 2001, First Officer Steve Scheibner packed his suitcase and waited for the phone call finalizing his assignment to fly American Airlines Flight 11, from Boston to Los Angeles. The call never came. His book *In My Seat* recounts the events leading up to Flight 11 and the subsequent death of Tom McGuinness in the seat that should have been filled by Steve Scheibner. (4)

Steve was signed up, all packed and ready to go the day before Flight 11 was scheduled to take off on September 11. However, a pilot with more seniority wanted the flight, so he was able to slip in just before the window of time closed for him to bump Scheibner.

What a sobering story of the sovereignty of God. Someone ended up dying in Steve's place just like Christ took the place of sinful mankind on the cross at Calvary. Jesus in turn took even the world's illnesses. God gave this American Airlines pilot another chance to live longer on this earth because another pilot took his place. This true story is a perfect symbol for New Testament, biblical theology.

I long to make the most out of every day, using every opportunity and grabbing every chance to share the good news of Christ's gospel. I want to live as if each day could be my last. I want to live a life of love for all my family and friends. I want to live life to the fullest. I want to leave a legacy. I want to leave it all on the field.

Suffering Can Be a Catalyst for Change

When you get a new lease on life, everything looks much different. I'm reminded of Charles Dickens's story *A Christmas Carol,* in which Scrooge is changed after all the visions he has from the ghosts. (5)

When he finally wakes up after his nightmarish, life-changing experience, he jumps out of bed and says, "I feel light as a feather." He throws open his window and yells out to a young boy to go buy him the biggest goose he can find and deliver it to Bob Cratchit's home for Tiny Tim. Scrooge now truly has a chance to leave a much better legacy behind than the one he was certainly headed for.

The Bible tells us about the transforming power of Christ's ability to change the sinful direction of one's life.

"Therefore, if anyone is in Christ, the new creation has come: The old has gone, the new is here!" (2 Corinthians 5:17).

The apostle Paul said, "I thank Christ Jesus our Lord, who has given me strength, that he considered me trustworthy, appointing me to his service. Even though I was once a blasphemer and a persecutor and a violent man, I was shown mercy because I acted in ignorance and unbelief. The grace of our Lord was poured out on me abundantly, along with the faith and love that are in Christ Jesus" (1 Timothy 1:12-14).

The ultimate purpose of Christ being on the cross was to take the wrath of God, reserved for the sins of the human race, by taking their place as the sacrifice due for their sins. It can be said that Jesus took our place of judgment so we could be free from the penalty of eternal death.

Anyone who receives this gift of redemption through Christ can say they are living on borrowed time because of Christ. Originally, you were not created to die a physical and spiritual death. Disobedience to God brought death and separation from God. Now anyone who receives Jesus as their Savior and Lord no longer has to die a spiritual death but gains eternal life.

Knowing you have eternal life can help soften the blows you take during times of suffering. Since you've recovered spiritually, God is able to give special peace, comfort, and strength to deal with physical challenges.

The Next Step on the Road to Recovery

Thus far I had survived eight days in the intensive care unit. Lo and behold, four days went by in the regular ward and my oxygen levels continued to stabilize. After a total of twelve days in the hospital, I was alert and not sleepy during the day, and my oxygen levels were getting good readings.

The doctors thought I could leave the hospital but believed I wasn't ready to come home yet. So they released me to a rehabilitation center that also served as a nursing home, so I could continue to get stronger, recuperate, and see what it might take for me to live back at home.

As I prepared to leave the hospital and head toward the rehab center/nursing home, I was certain I'd keep learning an abundance of things from suffering.

Suffering Develops the Genuineness of Your Faith

Suffering grief because of all kinds of trials is God's way of developing and proving the genuineness of your true faith and trust in Him. As gold is refined by fire, so too can your faith be refined by fire through suffering difficulties, trials, and testing, whether emotionally, mentally, or physically.

Here are numerous verses from throughout the Bible that reinforce this truth:

> In all this you greatly rejoice, though now for a little while you may have had to suffer grief in all kinds of trials. These have come so that the proven genuineness of your faith—of greater worth than gold, which perishes even though refined by fire, may result in praise, glory and honor when Jesus Christ is revealed. Though you have not seen him, you love him; and even though you do not see him now, you believe in him and are filled with an inexpressible and glorious joy. (1 Peter 1:6-8)

Isaiah tells us, "See, I have refined you, though not as silver; I have tested you in the furnace of affliction" (Isaiah 48:10).

You will have suffering, as Jesus said, "In this world you will have tribulations, but be of good courage, I have overcome the world of tribulations and will help you get through them too" (John 16:33).

We must go through many tribulations: "Confirming the souls of the disciples, and exhorting them to continue in the faith, and that we must through much tribulation enter into the kingdom of God" (Acts 14:22).

"The righteous cry out, and the L ORD hears them; he delivers them from all their troubles. The L ORD is close to the brokenhearted and saves those who are crushed in spirit" (Psalm 34:17-18).

These uncomfortable experiences called trials serve as a pressure cooker to develop our faith much like fire is used to melt and mold gold.

We must continue to remember that as long as we're on this earth, we are "not home yet." In this life we need God to be our shepherd to lead us, guide us, comfort us, and provide for us until we get to heaven.

CHAPTER 5

Not Home Yet

When I was told I could leave the hospital, I was glad but disappointed I could not go home. However, I was ready and willing to accept a new assignment and have the Lord write a new chapter with my life. It was still challenging not being able to go to my earthly home yet. I had been ready to go to heaven a few days earlier, which seemed much easier to accept than not being able to go home to my wife and family.

I went from thinking I was at death's door and prepared to enter heaven to sensing God whispering to my heart, "No, it's not time for you to enter heaven yet. I have more work for you to do on earth. So stay on the flight for further destinations."

We live our life of suffering between two worlds. We live in this world of suffering, but it's only for a while. How long that while actually is remains up to God. Heaven's clock runs on a different time zone. The Bible says, "With the Lord one day is as a thousand years and a thousand years as one day" (2 Peter 3:8 ESV). When one gets to heaven, everything that occurred on earth, good or difficult, will be a far and distant memory anyway.

I was forced to realize that because of my disability, I had to go to a rehabilitation nursing home to see how I would respond to the long-term use of the bi-pap machine and oxygen. I needed to build up my strength and endurance, along with learning how to operate a new, electric power chair. This was my new assignment, and though it was hard to accept, I would give it my best.

The Rehab Center/Nursing Home Presented Many Challenges

It is truly humbling to need the assistance of others to perform any of the daily essentials for living that most take for granted. At this time, I needed help getting into bed and out of my wheelchair with the aid of an electric lift. To do so, I am put in a mesh sling that is then attached to the electric lift machine. After it is in place, I am lifted out of bed and lowered into my wheelchair. All this was new as my post-polio-syndrome complications continued to slowly emerge.

Someone other than me had to put my pants on or take them off, along with my undergarments, shoes, and socks. On top of all this, I required someone to assist with a urinal and bedpan. To use the bedpan I needed two people, who were often hard to find.

I must admit I was worried about having to live too many days with long hours in bed without being able to get into my wheelchair for a greater part of the day. While in my power chair or scooter, I was able to get around, and live as normal a life as possible. Stuck in bed, I could not do much.

Most rehab or nursing centers can't afford to hire enough trained staff to give the individualized care that a person like me truly needs. This time was very trying for me. I felt as if I was facing overwhelming odds. When you cannot get out of bed on your own or are unable to move that much while lying down, you are totally dependent on others. This was the great drawback of being on my back at the hospital and then the rehabilitation center.

Sadly, it often became a game for me to press my call light button, which turned on a small colored light in the hall above my door. It was nerve-racking, counting the minutes it took to get an aide to come and assist me after I had touched my call button. The nursing home was far different from the hospital when it came to getting someone to respond to my call light.

Regularly, it was difficult for someone to drop what they were doing to come and help me for what I thought were legitimate needs. At times I could wait anywhere from fifteen minutes to an hour or more. I was truly trying to be patient and not complain even though it was very unnerving and challenging.

Many times I felt like a bother or was embarrassed because I needed help. Then when someone did finally come and I'd see they were stressed out and maybe doing a double shift and operating on exhaustion, I'd feel even worse, telling them what I needed.

As I said, I tried hard to be patient and hang in there until help arrived. I knew I could appear impatient or frustrated, so I tried to keep a good attitude and often prayed for the aides and nurses providing my care.

In the mornings I hoped someone would give me a sponge bath and take care of any pressure sores or apply lotion to the areas where my skin was uncomfortably dry. From lying and sitting a lot, I could easily get sores or abrasions that needed some type of cream or medicated lotion.

I also missed not being able to be placed on a shower chair and get under running water like I did at home. There were days when the aides were overwhelmed with trying to help everyone on their shift properly, so occasionally it would be difficult to get a full sponge bath.

Besides these inconveniences, only a nurse was allowed to operate the bi-pap machine and place the mask over me which covered my nose and mouth every night. Their policy was that no one other than a nurse could monitor the mask and bi-pap machine. This left out all the aides and other staff. Then a nurse was the only one allowed to remove the mask in the morning.

This was not always easy because every ward had one nurse on duty. There were a number of wards which meant three or four different nurses worked the various shifts. Every nurse was not familiar with me and it was difficult to teach each one how to use my bi-pap machine and mask properly. Every person has unique needs and wears one of many different types of masks. It's not one size fits all.

I realize a lot of this looks like complaining and being too picky. It is my earnest purpose to show, in as much detail as possible, the various trials and challenges that I had to face during this particular physical illness and its recovery. Most people do not truly understand or fathom what individuals with disabilities go through. I pray that my honesty and openness helps shed more light on how many others may be suffering. It would be wonderful if there were many more caregivers, aides, and resources available for those with physical and cognitive challenges.

A Few Weeks in Physical Therapy

Soon after I arrived at the rehabilitation nursing home, the physical therapy department sent three special rehab aides, or therapists, to get me into my power chair with an electric lift. They came usually by midmorning and helped me into my wheelchair so I could join the others at the physical therapy department.

The therapy determined was for my arm to be hooked up to electric stimulators on wirers attached to a machine. It was to activate muscle movement. Along with that I was given various rubber balls to squeeze and a few other hand exercise devices. I also spent the time in rehab learning how to operate my new power chair, which was guided by a digital board and a joystick for various functions. It was very complicated.

The only problem was that the rehab lasted only thirty to sixty minutes. Then I was sent back to my room with the rehab aides, who would wrap me on the sling attached to the lift and place me back in bed again, where I'd have to stay, helpless, for the rest of the day. On good days I was fortunate enough to stay in my power chair longer, when they agreed to my request to come back later to help me get into bed.

Therapy Benefits Ceased

We knew I could use the rehabilitation as long as our insurance covered it. After I had been going to the physical therapy department for two weeks, the administrators were told our insurance would no longer pay for it so we had to discontinue. There was still a lot more research and arrangements that had to be made regarding my future and where I'd go from here.

We were asked to pay out-of-pocket for the charges of room and board in advance for a month, which were quite expensive.

My wife and I, along with the family, were not ready to decide what to do next. My family did not yet know whether our home could feasibly accommodate me and what adjustments might be required.

They did not have enough resources to accurately estimate all the costs to schedule certified nurse's aides (CNA) and caregivers for home health care. Many more steps had yet to be covered in planning where I'd end up, whether it would be in a nursing home, assisted living center, or at home.

For the time being, I struggled to find enough regular floor aides available to get me onto the lift and into the power chair. The rehab aides could no longer assist me, which became a new source of frustration.

Suffering Can Be Emotionally Challenging

It was emotionally challenging for me to be so dependent on the regular assigned floor aides to get me out of bed and into my power chair. My regular floor aides were usually two people who had specific times for each room and covered maybe six to eight rooms or more, with two patients in each, on their shift. It was almost impossible to schedule enough time to reserve the lift and get into my power chair during my assigned time.

Usually when one aide came to see what I needed, I was told they'd be back when they found another aide to help. That took a lot more time too. They were often busy, understandably, but I'd have to wait a long time for enough help to get me out of bed and into the power wheelchair.

I know most nursing homes try to do their best to care for their residents. And the particular one I was in, I'm sure, endeavored to do their best. I'm thankful that I met many wonderful and caring nurses, aides, and staff there, even if I experienced numerous problems and unmet needs.

I imagine most nursing homes just cannot afford to pay enough certified nurse's aides or caregivers adequately to give the specialized individual and personal care that someone like me needed.

I definitely needed wisdom big time here. I prayed and prayed and prayed to be able to go home. Honestly, there were times I feared I'd never be able to live at home again. I was so emotionally stretched that at times I felt like I was caught in a nightmare.

Would life ever be normal again? Though my normal is far from most, at least it was as normal as mine could be. Prior to this health scare I had been able to come and go as I wished, see my wife every day in a home setting, visit with family and friends, go out to eat, attend a Chicago White Sox baseball game, go to the church for my pastoral ministry, and participate in worship services.

A Deeper Appreciation for Nursing Homes and Residents

I often visited parishioners who lived in nursing homes. Now I was rehabbing in one, unsure if or when I'd get home. It was emotional and trying, seeing all the elderly people often lined up, seated in wheelchairs along the walls. Many suffered from dementia and Alzheimer's; others had serious physical conditions too.

My unplanned medical emergency thrust me into being a resident of a nursing home at sixty years of age. Not even a month before this, I had been able to come and go as I wanted.

I had not been able to see my grandchildren while I was in the nursing home and saw them only once during the 12 days in the hospital. One was only six months old, and the other one was three.

They could have colds or be exposed to germs in the nursing home, so all I could do was look at their picture

I hung on my wall. That picture helped me get through all the days in the hospital and now here in the rehab center/nursing home.

Suffering Is an Unwelcome and Untimely Visitor

Out of nowhere, as if in fast forward, I was thrust into the future to feel what it was like being an elderly senior in a nursing home. What a shock to one's system. I was only sixty years old and was suddenly surrounded by seniors ten, twenty, thirty years older. It wasn't like I could get up and walk around on my own. I was confined to either a bed or a wheelchair.

I appreciate high-quality nursing homes, as they care for seniors suffering from numerous illnesses such as Alzheimer's and Parkinson's, and other physical and mental disabilities. I didn't want to come across as if I thought I deserved better or felt like I wasn't supposed to be in a place of this nature.

Naturally I had a hard time adjusting to the hospital and now a nursing home. It's not like I was at the age or had a lifestyle where I felt I needed to live in a retirement center.

I realized there were wonderful, loving, and caring individuals living within the walls of this nursing home. I'm sure the administrators and staff there felt they were all doing their best to take care of their residents. However, with my disability, I needed more hands-on, individualized care than most nursing homes can provide.

If it weren't for the countless nursing homes throughout America, what would happen to all the elderly and disabled? They play an important role in this subject of suffering. Whether it's a home for the elderly, a home for the disabled, an orphanage, or foster care, suffering is not an easy thing to deal with. Some places do a better job than others, yet all must continue to strive to care properly for whoever is in their care.

Suffering Behind Closed Doors of a Nursing Home

As a pastor I have visited numerous nursing homes to see elderly church members who had no one to care for them at home. I've conducted worship services, preached at nursing homes, and brought choirs to sing, especially during Christmas season.

Now I was a resident, listening to the residents cry out in pain day and night. I would see ambulances bring in new patients and take out patients who had passed away. Sick, hurting, lonely, and frightened senior citizens sitting in wheelchairs would often be lined up along the hallways. It was heart wrenching to see the sadness and pain in their eyes as I'd go by them in my motorized wheelchair. I did my best to be friendly and greet them with a smile. I often prayed for the residents, nurses, aides, and administrators.

Instead of coming as a visitor, I was one of them, just like that. A few weeks earlier I had been a vocational, full-time pastor at an active church. From living my life as an involved husband, father, and grandfather, I had become a resident in a nursing home, not really knowing if or when I'd be able to live at home again.

Startled by an Unplanned Visitor

I'll never forget one time, late at night, when an elderly woman was brought in by ambulance to our ward. The lights were off in the rooms, and out of nowhere, unknown to me, I saw what ended up being the new patient walk into our room. Apparently she had been left unattended for a few moments and wandered from her room. She began to move things around and startled my roommate, who was in his mid-seventies, as she talked to him.

She was going through his closet and taking things out, and he began to yell at her to leave his items alone. She was moving his wheelchair away from his bed and began grabbing him by the arm. I started to raise my voice and call out for help as loudly as I could by lifting my bi-pap mask from my mouth.

Finally an aide heard me and rushed to our room. She calmed down my roommate and attended to the woman. She was taken back to her new room. I knew she was confused and exhibiting signs of dementia or Alzheimer's. Needless to say, it was a hair-raising experience.

Suffering is a hard thing to deal with in our own humanness. I know no one really likes it or relishes it. As much of a challenge that suffering presents, it is a valuable tool God uses. As it goes, "Lord knows I've had my share."

An Avalanche of Suffering

Some are called to experience an avalanche of suffering that can last throughout ones whole life. Mine has been what could easily be referred to as "more than most could bear." There have been few breaks from aches, pains, or physical problems in my life.

I've had a lifetime to think about and reflect on sickness and suffering, blessings and burdens, fear and faith. Especially during the times it appeared things that happened in my life weren't fair, my faith has been continually stretched to help me keep seeing how God really does care and have our lives in His hands.

As hard as it may be to accept, God does have a specific will and plan for all those who believe in Him. God truly does have everything under control for His children even when it appears unfair. In the same way parents love each one of their children in a special way, God loves each of us.

Children often ask their parents, "Who do you love most?" When my kids asked me, I'd say, "I have no favorites. I love each of you very much in special and different ways." When I would allow the oldest to stay up later, or stay outside longer, the others would say, "That's not fair." What each one was or was not allowed had nothing to do with fairness or love. It all had to do with various times and situations.

Life's Not Fair; Some Suffer More Than Others

Sure, some suffer more than others, and that makes many ask questions about God being fair or not.

The answer to this falls in the "mysteries of God" category. God is God and doesn't need to give a reason or an answer for everything He does. Some questions and answers are best left to the truth that God has shown Himself to be a loving, caring, and compassionate almighty being. So when anything occurs that doesn't appear fair or right, leave it in God's hands and know He has a reason for allowing it.

"Will not the Judge of all the earth do right?" (Genesis 18:25).

"But our God *is* in heaven; He does whatever He pleases" (Psalm 115:3).

Throughout the Scriptures, all situations and circumstances reveal that God always has the best interest of His children in mind for whatever comes into their lives. There are secret things that only God knows about.

"The secret things belong to the LORD our God, but the things revealed belong to us and to our children forever, that we may follow all the words of this law" (Deuteronomy 29:29).

"For my thoughts are not your thoughts, neither are your ways my ways, declares the LORD. As the heavens, are higher than the earth, so are my ways higher than your ways and my thoughts, than your thoughts" (Isaiah 55:8-9).

There are circumstances that may look like a strange happening in time, an accident, or chance; though we know with God there are no occurrences outside His sovereign will and purpose. Still, some things look like they could fall in the "mysteries of God" category.

This verse falls into that category: "I returned and saw under the sun that—the race is not to the swift, nor the battle to the strong, nor bread to the wise, nor riches to men of understanding, nor favor to men of skill; But time and chance happen to them all" (Ecclesiastes 9:11).

There are many times when it appears that God falls asleep on the job. That He doesn't care. That He doesn't always deal with an individual fairly. To this I say God can deal with human beings in "strange and mysterious ways."

As I've made clear, God never promised this life would be fair. He doesn't plan the same exact life for each and every person. However, God does have a perfect plan for each and every person. This world is not all there is. As I've been saying, the fact is this planet we call Earth serves as more of a testing ground to develop our faith and belief in God.

We see this principle clearly revealed in the book of Daniel. There are two instances where it is clear that God is allowing Daniel and separately, Shadrach, Meshach, and Abednego, to go through a lion's den and a fiery furnace to test and develop their faith.

The three Hebrew young men were told to bow down and worship the image of the king. They would not and chose the punishment decreed by the king to be placed in a fiery furnace while Daniel's disobedience got him placed in a lion's den. I'm sure these young men were concerned and afraid, but their faith won out, and they accepted their fate.

Hoping God would do a miracle and deliver them, they still faced the fire and the lion's den being willing to die for their God. Was this fair? No! Yet God allowed it to happen for His glory. They were miraculously protected from the lions. They walked through the fire and yet were not burned.

"Shadrach, Meshach and Abednego replied to him, 'King Nebuchadnezzar, we do not need to defend ourselves before you in this matter. If we are thrown into the blazing furnace, the God we serve is able to deliver us from it, and he will deliver us from Your Majesty's hand. But even if he does not, we want you to know, Your Majesty that we will not serve your gods or worship the image of gold you have set up'" (Daniel 3:16-18).

Daniel was also told not to pray to anyone else but the image, and he was thrown into a den of lions. Daniel was human, and I'm sure his blood pressure went up and his heart was pounding. Still he spent a night, maybe eight hours, in a den of hungry lions.

> At the first light of dawn, the king got up and hurried to the lions' den. When he came near the den, he called to Daniel in an anguished voice, "Daniel, servant of the living God, has your God, whom you serve continually, been able to rescue you from the lions?"

Daniel answered, "May the king live forever! My God sent his angel and he shut the mouths of the lions. They have not hurt me, because I was found innocent in his sight. Nor have I ever done any wrong before you, Your Majesty."

The king was overjoyed and gave orders to lift Daniel out of the den. And when Daniel was lifted from the den, no wound was found on him, because he had trusted in his God." (Daniel 6:19-23)

Some are spared suffering, some have very little of it, others experience much suffering and find periods of relief, and a select few have to go through suffering for a long time with little relief. To paraphrase it: "God's ways are not our ways" (Isaiah 55:8).

Regardless of the difficulties and challenges that come to you, the best way to deal successfully with them is to have a deep faith in God and the Scriptures, along with cultivating a rock-solid positive attitude.

It's been said in one way or another, "The only negative and disabling thing in life is not having a positive attitude." Accept that life is not fair, get over it, and trust God to help you face suffering and afflictions head-on for His glory.

Living as an Ambassador for Christ

As we live our lives on the earth, fully committed and surrendered, we are encouraged to be an ambassador for God's kingdom. We must remember what an ambassador is. Ambassadors are representatives of one country living in another country, carrying out official business on their behalf.

"We are therefore Christ's ambassadors, as though God were making his appeal through us. We implore you on Christ's behalf: Be reconciled to God" (2 Corinthians 5:20).

"Dear friends, I urge you, as aliens and strangers in the world, to abstain from sinful desires, which war against your soul" (1 Peter 2:11).

The New Living Translation of this verse uses the term *temporary residents* for *aliens.* Believers in Christ are actually aliens, which means "from a different world."

Many preachers have shared the story of an old missionary couple returning home from their long time of ministry. It has inspired me often:

> After forty years of faithful service to the Lord as a missionary to Africa, Henry Morrison and his wife were returning to New York. As the ship neared the dock,

Henry said to his wife, "Look at that crowd. They haven't forgotten about us." However, unknown to Henry, the ship also carried President Teddy Roosevelt, returning from a big game hunting trip in Africa. Roosevelt stepped from the boat, with great fanfare, as people were cheering, flags were waving, bands were playing, and reporters waiting for his comment, Henry and his wife slowly walked away unnoticed. They hailed a cab, which took them to the one bedroom apartment which had been provided by the mission board.

Over the next few weeks, Henry tried, but failed to put the incident behind him. He was sinking deeper into depression when one evening, he said to his wife, "This is all wrong. This man comes back from a hunting trip and everybody throws a big party. We give our lives in faithful service to God for all these many years, but no one seems to care."

His wife cautioned him that he should not feel this way. Henry replied, "I know you're right, but I just can't help it. It just isn't right." His wife then said, "Henry, you know God doesn't mind if we honestly question Him. You need to tell this to the Lord and get this settled now. You'll be useless in His ministry until you do." Henry Morrison then went to his bedroom, got down on his knees and ... began pouring out his heart to the Lord. "Lord, you know our situation and what's troubling me. We gladly served you faithfully for years without complaining. But now God, I just can't get this incident out of my mind ..."

After about ten minutes of fervent prayer, Henry returned to the living room with a peaceful look on his face. His wife said, "It looks like you've resolved the matter. What happened?" Henry replied, "The Lord settled it for me. I told Him how bitter I was that the President received this tremendous homecoming, but no one even met us as we returned home. When I finished, it seemed as though the Lord put His hand on my shoulder and simply said, "But Henry, you are not home yet!" (1)

Christians are ambassadors, aliens and strangers on this earth. Therefore we should live as though "we're not home yet."

Suffering Gave Opportunities to Share Christ

During this long and arduous difficulty, I endeavored not to lose sight of how God was using it to provide opportunities for sharing with others about the person of Jesus Christ. There were many times I spoke to my aides, nurses, and therapists about my faith in Christ and the spiritual strength I was receiving from Him.

> Now I want you to know, brothers and sisters, that what has happened to me has actually served to advance the gospel. As a result, it has become clear throughout the whole palace guard and to everyone else that I am in chains for Christ. And because of my chains, most of the brothers and sisters have become confident in the Lord and dare all the more to proclaim the gospel without fear.

> It is true that some preach Christ out of envy and rivalry, but others out of goodwill. The latter do so out of love, knowing that I am put here for the defense of the gospel. The former preach Christ out of selfish ambition, not sincerely, supposing that they can stir up trouble for me while I am in chains. But what does it matter? The important thing is that in every way, whether from false motives or true, Christ is preached. And

because of this I rejoice. Yes, and I will
continue to rejoice. (Philippians 1:12-18)

For it has been granted to you on behalf
of Christ not only to believe in him, but
also to suffer for him. (Philippians 1:29)

Have you ever wondered how what you're going through
can actually be a blessing sent by God? This verse
found in Paul's letter to the Philippians came from him
to update the Christians there about the problems he
was going through.

This church actually sent one of their members to
visit him in prison. That's right, the apostle Paul was
in prison simply because he was preaching the gospel
of Jesus Christ.

He wasn't in the best of health, and his situation
was challenging, to say the least. On top of that, the
member of their church who came to bring him a gift
and some encouragement, Epaphroditus, was so ill
that he almost died.

But I think it is necessary to send back
to you Epaphroditus, my brother, co-
worker and fellow soldier, who is also your
messenger, whom you sent to take care
of my needs. For he longs for all of you
and is distressed because you heard he

was ill. Indeed he was ill and almost died.
But God had mercy on him, and not on
him only but also on me, to spare me
sorrow upon sorrow. Therefore I am all
the more eager to send him, so that when
you see him again you may be glad and I
may have less anxiety. So then, welcome
him in the Lord with great joy, and honor
people like him, because he almost died
for the work of Christ. He risked his life
to make up for the help you yourselves
could not give me. (Philippians 2:25-30)

Paul writes throughout this whole epistle how God was
using everything to advance the Good News of Jesus.
Let me remind you, God will use everything in your
life—trials, challenges, sufferings, and all the ups and
downs you face—to cause people to see Christ in your
situation and how you still "rejoice in the Lord always"
(Philippians 4:4).

I was able to share with numerous workers in the
rehab center/nursing home that I would pray for them.
It was my sincere prayer that they would come to have
a personal relationship with Jesus Christ.

I've always believed that God established His church
and its members to go out and share His message of
hope to a hurting world. Ravi Zacharius put it this way:
"The mission of the church is not only to bring people

to God but to take God to those who are wounded by the experiences of life, to touch those who are broken, to bring healing to those with damaged emotions. Those of us in the church recognize and accept our responsibility toward someone whose trust has been shattered, as evidenced by the schools, hospitals, rescue centers, and missions established by the church over the centuries" (2).

Determined to Leave the Nursing Home

We knew that for me to be able to get home, I'd need a number of caregivers working various shifts to make it work. My wife, as helpful and unbelievable as she is and has been to my life, had to stay working at her job as a high school technical assistant in the computer department. We needed her income and health insurance since I had to take a step down from my full-time job as a pastor because of this recent illness.

We wondered about affording caregivers so I could live at home. We knew it would be a matter of faith to trust God continually for the necessary funds home care would cost, if and when the doctors cleared me. But I was ready to take that step and hoped it would happen.

Would there be more complications? Would I continue to respond to the bi-pap machine for the sleep apnea?

Thank God I continued to improve and remain in good health.

Eventually it became clear that being able to come home was a matter of finances and finding the right affordable caregivers. We could also rely on the assistance from my family and friends to help keep the costs down. That along with a few furniture and room adjustments and I hoped I'd be able to come home, even though, nothing was sure yet.

The Lord was definitely teaching me, as I pieced various Scripture passages and experiences together, that I needed a new and broader definition and picture of what happiness is. I knew deep down that what the world believes happiness is differs from how God would define it. I was continuing to gain a deeper understanding about "the meaning of true happiness."

CHAPTER 6

The Meaning of True Happiness

Those who go through a lot of suffering and difficult times often deal with bouts of depression or moods. I can honestly say that if it weren't for my faith in God, I would not be able to deal or cope with life in as positive a manner as I have thus far.

People often ask others, "Are you happy?" That bothers me. Because of all the physical problems I've experienced, I tend to shy away from thinking in terms of happiness. Happiness speaks to me more about a feeling that's dependent on outward circumstances such as the weather, your bank account, your relationships, your physical health, your job, and so on.

Happiness comes and goes like the wind. Instead seek joy, which is an inner stability based on the foundation you have from building your life upon a personal relationship with Christ.

There's a tremendous verse that has helped me keep a positive attitude during life's challenges. It's found in Nehemiah 8:10, which says, "The joy of the Lord is your strength." Knowing God intimately anchors your life in the "joy of the Lord." It fosters an emotion of security that your life is not based on circumstances; to the contrary it's established on the truth that God is leading and directing your life no matter what happens.

I regularly reflect on the saying "When you can't trace God's hand, trust His heart." It means terrible and difficult things may happen in your life that can cause you to wonder where God's hand of guidance and protection is. In all reality, His hand is sometimes hard to see.

The Bible reveals the heart of God as one of compassion, love, grace, and mercy. When hard times come, you can trust that God has your best interests in mind. He can be trusted to stay with you whether or not you can see evidence of it.

In the famous poem called "Footprints in the Sand," the writer had a dream type vision and saw times when there were two sets of footprints in the sand as she went through life, symbolizing hers and God's.

Yet when she faced the worst times, there was only one set of prints. This troubled her, so she asked God why there was only one set of footprints during the tough times. God responded, "That's when I carried you" (1).

So when suffering or bad things happen, you can rest securely in the truth that if your life is surrendered to the will of God, He guides, guards, and guarantees that you'll be kept securely in the palm of His hand.

Jesus prayed, "Holy Father, protect them by the power of your name, the name you gave me, so that they may be one as we are one. While I was with them, I protected them and kept them safe by that name you gave me. None has been lost ... Father, I want those you have given me to be with me where I am, and to see my glory, the glory you have given me because you loved me before the creation of the world" (John 17:11-12, 24).

Need More Than Happiness During Suffering

Trials and difficulties often threaten your sense of security. That's why it is essential to base your life on firm spiritual principles found in the Bible. When your life is built on the truth you'll be able to face problems head-on.

As a pastor, I've often heard this one-liner about a troubled married couple: "We're not making each other happy anymore, so we're getting a divorce." Like one person is supposed to make you happy for the rest of your life. That's an unrealistic expectation to put on anyone. A healthy marriage means having two partners more concerned about caring for their partner than themselves.

Having a genuine relationship with a loving, caring, and forgiving God will give you true joy. Building a life that is committed to loving and obeying God and His word results in an abiding joy that comes from the confidence one has in knowing everything in one's life is in God's control, whether in good times or tough times.

A believer's life can and should be built on loving God no matter what. Christ shared the two greatest commandments. The Jewish religious leaders called the first one the Shema. It says, "You shall love the Lord your God with all your heart, with all your soul, and with your entire mind. This is the first and great commandment. And the second is like it: 'You shall love your neighbor as yourself.' On these two commandments hang all the Law and the Prophets" (Matthew 22:39-40).

This passage should be the seedbed of everyone's being. The bottom line of living a life like this dispels the notion that you must seek happiness in life. If happiness is your barometer for life, you'll go up and down with grave disappointment. By seeking God and not happiness, you will be able to stand up stronger whenever you face times of suffering.

Basing your life on loving God with your all will definitely fill your life with joy. I like what Dr. James Emery White said about C. S. Lewis:

When Lewis wrote of the awakening of his own heart, he would often describe it in terms of being "surprised by joy." "Joy" for Lewis was the holy grail of life. It was what made the great Norse legends so appealing to him as a boy. Through them he would catch glimpses of something beyond him, transcendent of the human experience, and knew such was the longing of his heart. I am sure you know of the difference between happiness and joy. Happiness is circumstantial; joy is foundational. Happiness has to do with what I feel; joy is who I am. Happiness is cheap; joy is priceless. For Lewis, the joy he longed for was God. (2)

Happiness can come and go with your circumstances. Joy can be consistent and stable regardless of whether you're experiencing mountain peaks or valleys.

The God of the Valley

I Kings 20:28 shares a time when Elijah told the king of Israel about the God of the valley. "The man of God came up and told the king of Israel, 'This is what the Lord says: Because the Arameans think the Lord is a god of the hills and not a god of the valleys, I will deliver this vast army into your hands, and you will know that I am the Lord.'"

Although most people naturally look for mountaintop experiences, we can gain the character qualities God desires for our lives only while we are in the valley. It is in the valley where the fruit is planted and harvested. It cannot grow on the mountain; it must grow in the valley.

Granted, God is a God of the mountain, but He is even more a God of the valley. When two prophets, Moses and Elijah, appeared to three apostles who were with Jesus on the mountaintop, they wanted to stay and not return to the valley. In the valley, it is more difficult to see very far ahead because of the terrain, mist, and fog; the clouds often cover the valley and limit the sight.

Joseph was thrust into a deep valley that left him wondering if the God of his father had forsaken him when he was delivered to Egypt. Jesus hoped that He might be able to avoid the valley that caused Him to sweat blood in the garden (Matthew 26:39). There is a valley that each of us must enter, usually unwillingly, to experience the God of the valley.

Jesus even felt His Father had forsaken Him in the valley of the cross when His own human nature rose up with His divine nature and He cried, "My God, my God, why have you forsaken me?" (Psalm 22:1, Matthew 27:6)

There are times in the valley when God seems distant and not even there. Those are the times where true faith is exercised and developed.

Living in this world is like seeing your face dimly through a fogged-up mirror or broken glass. "For now we see in a mirror, but then face to face. Now I know in part, then I shall know fully, even as I have been fully known" (1 Corinthians 13:12 [ESV]).

There will come a time when we will see and understand all the reasons behind suffering and evil in this broken and fallen world. Until then we must travel this life with the Bible as our road map. The holy Scriptures are there to light the way to navigate the challenges we face. "Your word is a lamp to my feet and a light to my path" (Psalm 119:105 [ESV]).

Suffering Can Lead You to a Different Perspective

When you have a personal relationship with Christ, everything about your life changes: your goals, desires, and ambitions. All your commitments take on a higher calling. Even suffering seems to have a different purpose and meaning.

No longer do you grasp at certain creature comforts or material things to make you happy. Your life takes on an inner passion that wants to allow everything in your life to give God glory.

An often-quoted statement by C. S. Lewis bears repeating here: "God whispers to us in our pleasures, speaks in our conscience, but shouts in our pain: it is His megaphone to rouse a deaf world." He goes on to say God uses pain to, "plant the flag of truth within the fortress of a rebel soul." (3) God has used my suffering to get my attention regularly.

A major purpose of suffering is to show forth the glory of God in our lives. We find this clearly illustrated in the Gospel of John about the man born blind.

> As he went along, he saw a man blind from birth. His disciples asked him, "Rabbi, who sinned, this man or his parents, that he was born blind?"
>
> "Neither this man nor his parents sinned," said Jesus, "but this happened so that the works of God might be displayed in him. As long as it is day, we must do the works of him who sent me. Night is coming, when no one can work. While I am in the world, I am the light of the world."
>
> After saying this, he spit on the ground, made some mud with the saliva, and put it

> on the man's eyes. "Go," he told him, "wash
> in the Pool of Siloam" (this word means
> "Sent"). So the man went and washed,
> and came home seeing. (John 9:1-7)

God used this man's blindness to give Him glory, as He used him to show forth His grace, mercy, and power. This passage reveals some of the thoughts about sickness many Jews of Jesus' day had. They may have picked this up from their religious leaders. Specifically, many Jewish rabbis and scholars believed that physical or mental illness was a sign of punishment for sinning or doing something wrong, whether committed by the sufferer or by a family member.

Granted, the Bible does reveal instances when God sent an illness, plague, or tragedy as a direct result of sin, disobedience, or rebellion. (See Exodus 32:25-35.) On the other hand, sickness or tragedy often comes not because of someone's sin but to show a deeper purpose or to act as an opportunity for God to perform a miracle or teach something much deeper.

Important to See Yourself as God Does

Bestselling author, John Mason said, "You were born an original. Don't die a copy."

Wow! What a true statement. God knit us together in our mother's womb to be uniquely one of a kind.

Scripture says, "For you created my inmost being; you knit me together in my mother's womb. I praise you because I am fearfully and wonderfully made; your works are wonderful, I know that full well" (Psalm 139:13-14).

Why do so many of us want to copy someone else? When you get to Heaven, God won't say, "Why weren't you like so-and-so?"

You were created to be yourself, the gifted person God wants you to be, conformed to the image of Jesus Christ, redeemed and renewed by His Spirit.

An individual with a disability, whether it's physical, cognitive, or both, usually has a hard time accepting and believing that God created them for a reason. It is understandably difficult for those of us with disabilities to embrace the belief that we are unique, special, one-of-a-kind individuals.

I know how difficult it was for me to accept my deformities and physical limitations. As a teenager I desperately wanted to fit in with the cool crowd. Yet I had a severely deformed right arm that was quite obvious to all.

I walked with a serious limp, and my scoliosis caused me to bend over as I took steps. Sure, I was glad I could walk, even if it was only for short distances.

Still, I wanted to run, jump, roll on the ground, and pop to my feet. Yet the closest I came to that was in my dreams.

I'll never forget when I was eighteen years of age, telling a neighborhood girl that I wanted to take her on a date. She told me, "Ken, you're a nice guy and I am glad we're friends, but I can't date you because you're crippled."

My heart got stuck in my throat and I could hardly keep talking. I dropped her off in my car and drove home crying all the way. I thought, *Why did God make me so ugly?* I felt like the Hunchback of Notre Dame in France, Quasimodo, like the *Phantom of the Opera*, like the prince turned into a frog looking for true love to break the spell in the Disney film *The Princess and the Frog.*

It was not easy having a disability while I was growing up, or for that matter, at any time in my life. Then something happened, a game changer. I came to know Jesus Christ as my personal Savior and Lord.

I began to relax more and accept that I could be the person God designed me to be—the original, not a copy. I felt better about myself in that if God created me like I was, He must have had a purpose and reason behind it.

Moses was told by God to speak to Pharaoh of Egypt to let His people go. But Moses complained that he had a disability. He said he had a speech impediment and stuttered terribly so he couldn't do what God told him to.

God wouldn't take that as an excuse. In Exodus 4:11 God says, "Who has made man's mouth? Who makes him mute, or deaf, or seeing, or blind? Is it not I, the Lord?" God allows some to suffer with a disability to show forth His glory and strength through their lives.

The disciples heard Jesus say that a man was born blind to show forth the glory of God in John 9. The apostle Paul knew about this, as he suffered with a "thorn in the flesh" that God would not remove in order to "show that His strength is made perfect in weakness" (2 Corinthians 12:7-11). Paul brought glory to God in all his sufferings.

I finally came to the place where I could surrender my disability to the Lord and learn to praise Him despite my suffering. I began to give God the glory and praise with my life in whatever I could do for Him. I knew God wanted to use me to show forth His power and strength.

It was a life-changing experience to be able to echo the words of Philippians 4:13, "I can do all things through him (Christ) who strengthens me."

Biblical Joy Gives Strength for Suffering

Nehemiah 8:10 speaks of a joy that is not a feeling as much as a calm, peaceful, emotional balance that fills your soul because of your secure position in a solid relationship with God.

This joy comes from God, not from money or materialism, or good times or good circumstances. Feelings come and go, but a personal relationship with Jesus Christ will cause an everlasting joy. That's why the apostle Paul was able to face a lifetime of tough circumstances and suffering.

Happiness must not be based on receiving a miracle healing, or having an easier life. Anyone can be happy when they receive blessings and good things. What really makes a difference is depending on "the joy of the Lord," regardless of how tough your circumstances may be.

Suffering Can Be Used by God to Discipline

Most of us do not have a hard time believing that bad things can happen when we do something wrong. We probably feel like God caught us with our hands in the cookie jar when suffering, problems, or accidents happen.

In any event, whenever suffering does happen to come, it's not a bad idea to ask God to reveal whether He's using it as a means of discipline to get your attention.

We all go through times where blind spots can cause us to drift off the center of God's will.

Often whenever God's children got off course, He disciplined them with illness or difficulties. "But they soon forgot what he had done and did not wait for his plan to unfold. In the desert they gave in to their craving; in the wilderness they put God to the test. So he gave them what they asked for, but sent a wasting disease among them" (Psalm 106:13-15).

Consequently, often in His will, whenever they cried out to Him, He "sent His word and healed them" (Psalm 107:20). Then they were restored when they believed and obeyed His Word.

Psalm 119:67 tells us that King David acknowledged that his affliction drove Him to restore his relationship with God: "Before I was afflicted I went astray, but now I obey your word."

Suffering and challenges were sent by God to the early church in Corinth because they were abusing and incorrectly celebrating the Holy Communion. We see an enlightening Scripture in 1 Corinthians 11:23-30 where we read the following:

> For I received from the Lord what I also passed on to you: The Lord Jesus, on the night he was betrayed, took bread, and

when he had given thanks, he broke it and said, "This is my body, which is for you; do this in remembrance of me." In the same way, after supper he took the cup, saying, "This cup is the new covenant in my blood; do this, whenever you drink it, in remembrance of me." For whenever you eat this bread and drink this cup, you proclaim the Lord's death until he comes.

So then, whoever eats the bread or drinks the cup of the Lord in an unworthy manner will be guilty of sinning against the body and blood of the Lord. Everyone ought to examine themselves before they eat of the bread and drink from the cup. For those who eat and drink without discerning the body of Christ eat and drink judgment on themselves. That is why many among you are weak and sick, and a number of you have fallen asleep.

New Testament theologian, Dr. Gordon Fee, whom I had the privilege of meeting and listening to said, "This is a very sobering passage that comes with a warning of suffering God's discipline for improperly partaking of Communion in an inappropriate manner. Church history records that many of the church religious leaders and members over-imbibed the wine, even becoming drunk, not leaving enough for the congregation. God allowed some of the offenders to become weaker, others got sick and sadly, a few even died prematurely." (5)

God does reserve the right to discipline His children, as we see in Hebrews 12:7-13:

> Endure hardship as discipline; God is treating you as his children. For what children are not disciplined by their father? If you are not disciplined—and everyone undergoes discipline—then you are not legitimate, not true sons and daughters at all. Moreover, we have all had human fathers who disciplined us and we respected them for it. How much more should we submit to the Father of spirits and live! They disciplined us for a little while as they thought best; but God disciplines us for our good, in order that we may share in his holiness. No discipline seems pleasant at the time, but painful. Later on, however, it produces a harvest of righteousness and peace for those who have been trained by it. Therefore, strengthen your feeble arms and weak knees. "Make level paths for your feet," so that the lame may not be disabled, but rather healed.

God's discipline has a purpose, a reason, and a desired result to draw people back to Him or to teach important spiritual lessons. God doesn't allow tragedy, accidents, illness, or suffering for no reason. Christ is a compassionate, gracious, and merciful almighty being, who desires everyone to know Him, His forgiveness, and redemption.

Consider this passage: "He is patient with you, not wanting anyone to perish, but everyone to come to repentance" (2 Peter 3:9).

These lifelong spiritual lessons took on a deeper and more meaningful perspective for me after I had suffered from this life-threatening illness. With all the suffering I'd already gone through, I thought I knew almost all there was to know about it. I realize that with God, there's always something more to learn about as He teaches us through suffering.

"So then, those who suffer according to God's will should commit themselves to their faithful Creator and continue to do good" (1 Peter 4:19). I obviously knew I was in God's will to go through what I had just suffered and realistically, all that I have suffered thus far in my life. I am thankful that I've been able to commit myself to our faithful Creator and continue to do His will.

Suffering Is Used as God's Pruning Shears

God often uses suffering to serve as pruning shears in the hands of a gifted gardener. I am always amazed by what individuals with a green thumb can do to trees, plants, flowers, and gardens. They can take withering, almost dead vegetation and bring it back to life.

A general definition of pruning from professional gardeners is "cutting off leaves or branches within limits in order to remove dead or diseased foliage or branches. It is used to control or direct growth, increase the quality or yield of flowers or fruit, and to ensure the growth position of main branches to enhance structural strength" (6).

Jesus speaks of God, the Father as a divine gardener for the soul:

> I am the true vine, and my Father is the gardener. He cuts off every branch in me that bears no fruit, while every branch that does bear fruit he prunes so that it will be even more fruitful. You are already clean because of the word I have spoken to you. Remain in me, as I also remain in you. No branch can bear fruit by itself; it must remain in the vine. Neither can you bear fruit unless you remain in me. (John 15:1-4)

Every branch that bears fruit needs pruning so it can remain healthy and bear more fruit. This analogy holds true for the way God uses suffering.

Whenever a believer suffers from an illness, accident, tragedy, or difficulty, they should say, "Lord, what are you trying to teach me? Father, what might I need to look at regarding my spiritual life? Am I spending enough time with you in prayer? Am I reading and studying your word openly and as often as I should? Are my priorities in order? Have I been living with a heart of forgiveness between You and others?"

These and other similar questions must be considered during times of suffering. Whether the suffering is temporary, for a season, or for a lifetime with a permanent chronic illness or disability, it is a dynamic tool in God's hand for developing spiritual growth and more Christ-like people.

I can hear some of you saying, "I have all the character I need. I've gone through enough now, Lord. Please give me a break." Sadly, it doesn't work that way. For some strange reason, God chooses certain of His children to experience an unbelievable amount and length of time suffering. Often it is a mystery, and the Lord usually does not offer a clear reason why.

I myself am in this latter category. Has my life been easy? No. Does it seem fair? No. I didn't write this book to get sympathy or to paint myself as some kind of martyr or super-saint. I felt led to show all the things I've had to deal with to reveal what God's grace and power can help a believer endure.

Suffering Can Chip Away at Your Hope

Prolonged suffering can have a way of chipping away at your hope. This illness that put me in the hospital and rehabilitation center was stretching over thirty days and became my longest stay in recent memory. I longed to be able to get back home. Proverbs 23:10 tells us, "Hope deferred makes the heart sick, but a longing fulfilled is a tree of life."

Emotionally I kept praying that somehow God would work it out that enough finances would be available to pay for personal home caregivers and all the rest of our bills. This seemed like such an uphill battle that I was afraid I'd never get home.

In the rehab center minutes seemed like hours, hours seemed like days, days seemed like weeks. I never lost hope, and I knew God had kept me alive for a reason. It was no accident that I had survived this health scare. I knew God was working in my life for a reason and had a plan that would unfold step by step.

In my humanness I sometimes cried out, "How much longer, God? How much more can I take?" Of course

I knew God was with me and had everything under control. But I was having what I call a "John the Baptist moment."

When John the Baptist was arrested by Herod and placed in prison, it appeared that the delay of his seeing Christ usher in the kingdom of God may have gotten to him. He believed in Christ. He knew deep down Christ was the Messiah.

Doubt may have been creeping in just a bit. John the Baptist was ready to die for his faith in Jesus. In a moment of weakness, as can happen to any believer in Christ, John sent his disciples to ask Jesus again if He was the one he thought he was.

"John's disciples told him about all these things. Calling two of them, he sent them to the Lord to ask, 'Are you the one who is to come, or should we expect someone else?'" (Luke 7:18-19).

Jesus patiently and lovingly told John the Baptist's disciples to assure him He was who He said He was.

"So he (Jesus) replied to the messengers, 'Go back and report to John what you have seen and heard: The blind receive sight, the lame walk, those who have leprosy are cleansed, the deaf hear, the dead are raised, and the good news is proclaimed to the poor. Blessed is anyone who does not stumble on account of me'" (Luke 7:22-23).

I'm sure John the Baptist was then reassured and God strengthened him to face his judgment that the queen wanted "his head on a platter." John was able to face his suffering for "the glory of God."

In any event, God was continuing to get my attention. God's unlimited outpouring of grace, mercy, and comfort kept me on an even keel of thanksgiving and praise to Him for keeping me alive to do more work for His glory.

Winston Churchill said, "The farther backward you can look the farther forward you are likely to see" (7).

I believe "looking back" at your past helps you realize you've arrived at where you are now. This shows that if God got you through all you've experienced in the past, He'll get you through today and whatever comes tomorrow.

CHAPTER 7

Looking Back

How did I get here so suddenly? It seems like only yesterday I was a young, stronger, energetic man with a vision, and filled with passion. Where did the time go? I often heard my grandparents and parents say, "Time sure goes by fast." Now here I am, thinking the same thing.

For most of my life I was able to walk, drive a car, and pretty much do everything I needed to with the assistance that my wife and sons were able to provide. I used a wheelchair only when I had to go long distances. At home and in the church I could walk and get around with no problem.

However, in recent years it seems as though I've been in the fight of my life, trying to make adjustments to live as normally as possible. Thank God my faith in the Lord is still strong and my passion to serve Him wholeheartedly continues to drive me.

I often hold on to a promise in the book of Proverbs: "Trust in the Lord with all your heart and lean not on your own understanding; in all your ways submit to him, and he will make your paths straight" (Proverbs 3:5-6).

Suffering Often Causes You to Look Back at the Past

It wasn't until about ten years ago that I began to decline slowly. I could tell something was changing physically. It led me to have tests performed by the Northwestern Memorial Neurological Department, a major hospital in Chicago. The results revealed I was suffering from post-polio syndrome. I couldn't believe it. I thought I had already overcome and dealt with that ugly disease as an infant.

I was able to make it through childhood and adapted well. I handled the ups and downs of high school and the teenage years. I dove head first into my early college years and figured I was on my way to putting the effects of polio behind me.

I tackled a high-quality biblical education in which I earned college and seminary degrees. I got married by the time I was twenty-five and raised a family of four sons. I was privileged to hold pastoral roles at quite a few churches and founded a nonprofit ministry called 'Til Healing Comes Ministries.

Post-Polio Syndrome Caused Many Complications

Polio did not stop me from being a highly motivated and driven person, determined to accomplish as much as possible, even though I had a challenging physical handicap.

These are some of the major obstacles that could have kept me from achieving a marriage, family, and a career:

I was unable to stand up from any seated position, whether on a bed or chair. I always had to ask someone to help me get to a standing position. I could stand up on my own if it was a stool, because of its higher position. If I had to be alone at home, I often sat on a stool. I was never able to climb stairs unassisted.

I required help getting dressed and undressed, with braces on my left leg and back. For quite a while I could put on my own socks and full-length steel leg brace with leather straps and buckles. I needed help putting on my shoes and tying them, along with getting my shirt buttoned or pulled over my head.

I could wash my hair in the sink, and as long as I was helped on and off the commode, I could be virtually on my own the rest of the day. It ended up being a lifelong trick to limit my bowel movements to once a day and in the morning, right after breakfast. Thankfully most days went fine. But this would be one of the most inconvenient things throughout my life.

Now I have to be lifted onto the commode by an electric lift that uses a sling under my legs, back, and arms. It lifts me while seated in the wheelchair and lowers me onto the commode that is set over the toilet.

Finally, in the past I just needed assistance bathing, as I could stand and pivot to sit on a shower chair that was placed in the bathtub where my wife assisted me regularly.

Currently the electric lift has to place me on a bath commode with wheels that is rolled into a wheel-in shower. It takes two caregivers to assist me with this.

We knew challenges lay ahead for me in the future. But just what those would be, no one knew. Still we keep forging ahead, trusting God to give us the strength and courage to go forward for His glory.

The apostle Paul lived his life in such a way that he kept his life pressing forward: "I press on toward the goal to win the prize for which God has called me heavenward in Christ Jesus" (Philippians 3:14).

Defining Post-Polio Syndrome

What's this thing called post-polio? It appears that some victims who succumbed to the polio virus, which attacked the central nervous system and caused damage to the spine that controlled the muscular system, suffered more weakness and complications as they aged. It usually begins to show itself when one is in their late forties to early fifties and even sixties.

Post-polio syndrome raised its ugly head when I was in my early fifties. I began falling more, my legs were getting weaker, and it was more difficult to drive my van. I had been able to drive with no problem since I was eighteen years old. But now, it was getting harder to perform certain physical things.

Wikipedia describes the syndrome in this way:

> After a period of prolonged stability individuals who had been infected and recovered from polio begin to experience new signs and symptoms, characterized by muscular atrophy (decreased muscle mass), weakness, pain and fatigue in limbs that were originally affected or in limbs that didn't seem to have been affected at the time of the initial polio illness. Post-Polio Syndrome is a very slowly progressing condition marked by periods of stability followed by new declines in the ability to carry out usual daily activities.

Most patients become aware of their decreased capacity to carry out daily routines due to significant changes in mobility, decreasing upper limb function and lung capability. Fatigue is often the most disabling symptom; even slight exertion often produces disabling fatigue and can also intensify other symptoms. Problems breathing or swallowing, sleep-related breathing disorders, such as sleep apnea and decreased tolerance for cold temperatures are other notable symptoms.

Increased activity during intervening healthy years between the original infection and onset of PPS can amplify the symptoms. Thus, contracting poliomyelitis at a young age can result in particularly disabling PPS symptoms. (1)

Sadly, as I began to experience symptoms of post-polio syndrome, I had to fight against worry, anxiety, and discouragement. Obviously this is nothing new to me, but it does get old when you constantly think, *What now? Why did this have to happen? It's not fair to always go through so many trials and troubles. I don't know anyone else who's had to go through as much as me.*

As a minister and person of faith, I knew deep down that God would help me deal with any new type of suffering and difficulties. Still, in my humanness and frailties, I battled to stay on top of any negative or depressing feelings.

I had to accept that even though my problems are not life threatening, they can be debilitating and challenging. I was told that one can usually keep up with one's normal activities and employment until serious changes present themselves. Onward, I continued to march for the glory of God.

Let's Go All The Way to the Beginning of My Suffering

Let me look back to the beginning of my battle with polio. It began when I was only fourteen months old back in 1952. Born a perfectly healthy baby on July 31, 1951, I was the firstborn child of my parents. In 1952, 60,000 people in the United States were infected with the polio virus.

Wikipedia defines polio in this way:

> Polio, or poliomyelitis, is an infectious viral disease that can strike at any age and affects a person's nervous system. Between the late 1940s and early 1950s, polio crippled around 35,000 people each

year in the United States alone, making it one of the most feared diseases of the twentieth century.

The polio vaccine was first introduced in 1955; its use since then has eradicated polio from the United States. The World Health Organization reports polio cases have decreased by more than 99 percent since 1988, from an estimated 350,000 cases then, to 1,352 reported cases in 2010. As a result of the global effort to eradicate the disease, only three countries (Afghanistan, Nigeria, and Pakistan) remain polio-endemic as of February 2012, down from more than 125 in 1988. (2)

As you can see, polio was an epidemic as a virus for many, many years. It was a dreaded disease that could close down swimming pools, water fountains, parks, and schools. A person would be healthy one day and then contract the polio virus and exhibit a high fever and become listless, motionless, and very ill.

Before the polio vaccination discovered by Dr. Jonas Salk in 1955, polio victims would be quarantined for a number of weeks, as they were extremely contagious. That is the time when the virus would do its dirty work, and no two people would exhibit the same aftereffects.

Some victims may have been left with one leg shorter than the other and/or with weakened arms and/or legs. Others more seriously affected had weakened diaphragm and lung muscles and could not breathe on their own; they were placed in an iron lung ventilator machine.

Other individuals like me may show effects throughout their whole bodies. I received a curvature of the spine, a weakened and deformed right arm, a weakened left arm, and weakness in both my right and left legs. I could walk, slowly with the aid of a leg brace, but not for great distances. I walked for maybe fifty to a hundred feet and then had to rest a moment or so. I could stand for a long time, although I needed to lean on something to help my balance.

I would often lose my balance and fall to the ground. Sometimes I cut my head open and needed stitches at the hospital or doctor's office.

With this type of disability I was no stranger to doctors, and spent many long hours at the doctor's office for examinations, X-rays, and tests. I was hospitalized frequently as a child because I had to undergo numerous major surgeries along with experimental casts and braces. My mother and father tirelessly invested their lives and resources into my well being.

It was often very difficult. I had my moments of sadness and questioning why me. However, surprisingly I had a spirit of optimism and positively adapted to my handicap and environment. I was, overall, a happy kid and loved God, my family, friends, school, sports, music, movies, and much more.

Suffering and Pressures on the Family

It's hard to express the emotions a person with a disability has when it comes to the family. In many cases the one who is disabled needs assistance just to make it day to day. Whether it's a physical or emotional disability or both, each situation puts pressure and demands on the family.

There is also stress on the person who's disabled. It was painful to feel like I was a bother. At times I felt frustrated that family members had to drop things or put things on hold to help me.

Some are born with a disability, others get a disease, and of course accidents can cause impairments. Whatever the case, unless the disability is serious enough to cause long-term hospitalization or specialized care from some type of live-in care center, the family is usually the first set of caregivers.

My mother and father got me bathed and dressed, assisted with toiletries, and helped me get around through grade school, high school, and some junior college. Each sibling, as they got older, pitched in to help me too.

Desired to Live as Normally as Possible

I did everything I could to live as normal a life as possible. Would I ever be able to be totally independent? No, but I hoped I could lead a productive and fulfilling life with the assistance of loving parents, brothers, and sisters.

Then as I got older, I hoped for help from good friends and possibly, a loving wife, as amazing as that would be. I dreamt I'd be fortunate enough to have children and grandchildren. This was a deep dream in my heart as a young teenage boy hoping and praying.

Faced Painfully Embarrassing Situations in Childhood

One of the most challenging physical limitations my disability imposed upon me when it came time to go to school and get out of the house was in the personal area of the bowel movement. I was a pro at trying to hold a bowel movement. I did my dead level best to go first thing in the morning right after breakfast. But Mother Nature occasionally did not cooperate, causing extra stress and problems.

I never forgot one such day in the fifth grade when I just couldn't hold my bowel movement until I got home. I was usually able to wait until I got home after my mother or father picked me up.

I'll never forget one day in the fifth grade when I just couldn't wait until my mother picked me up. The physical function that other kids could take care of in a quick trip to the bathroom became unbearable and my usual tactic of trying to concentrate on something else failed. My classmates were smirking and looking around as kids will, asking each other who was the guilty party.

Eventually I worked up enough nerve to ask a friend nearby to go tell the teacher to call my mother to come and pick me up right away. It felt like the clock crawled and time stood still.

Finally, my mother arrived and I whispered what had happened. She helped lift me to a standing position out of the chair. When I stood, some fecal material fell down my leg and hit the floor.

No way would I wear a diaper as a fifth-grade kid, even if it left me a prime candidate for mishaps like this. I'd take my chances. Mom got me home, cleaned me up, and did her best to comfort me.

I had to be a tough-minded, well-balanced child to cope with a challenging disability. After that most embarrassing circumstance, I went to school the next day and did what my father always told me to do. I could hear him say, "keep a stiff upper lip and get back in the game. It's fourth down and inches to the goal line, and we're going for it." He often encouraged me with football-type language.

I did not want to attend a school strictly for children with disabilities because I desired to live like any other kid, have neighborhood friends, and grow up learning to live in the normal world. There was no inclusion procedure for local schools that made it mandatory to accommodate special needs students.

I didn't start out owning or using a wheelchair; that came when I was a teenager. Before that, my neighborhood friends would push me around in a red wagon that had a homemade wooden seat on the back with a couple of two-by-fours on each side extending up the back so they could push me while I steered.

My mother drove a car and took me to and from grade school in the Mount Greenwood section of Chicago almost every day for eight years. At times a few of the older boys pushed me to school in my red wagon.

Left Sitting Alone in Class During Recess

My grade-school years had their ups and downs because of my disability. I had many difficult adjustments to make. A tough situation occurred every day during recess when all the students went outside to play kickball, jump rope, throw a football, or play catch with a softball. I was left sitting in the classroom all by myself, watching them play through the window, during my whole grade-school experience, grades one through eight.

I remember tears would often well up in my eyes as I watched all the other kids having fun while I was left all alone in a quiet, lonely classroom. Amazingly, I still kept a positive disposition and developed numerous friendships with fellow classmates.

I have a number of fond memories of my grade-school years, such as being a batboy for a local community Little League team. Sure, no teams really had an official batboy, but my father made sure the Falcons, coached by a friend of his, had a batboy who received his own uniform.

I was able to play outside in the immediate neighborhood on a limited basis, but managed to find a few things to do. I often competed in baseball and was a good hitter and pitcher, and played the field a little. At times I'd sit on a stool and be a designated hitter, way before professional American League teams had one. But I had something else unique: a designated runner.

Although I had sufferings and challenges in childhood learning to deal with the physical deformities from polio, I always had a profound and deep love for Jesus Christ. My faith played a very important part in my family and personal life.

Grandpa said, "It could be worse. Remember the *Titanic*."

My father's mother, Mary, immigrated to America from southern Ireland in the early 1900s, as did his father, Patrick. This grandfather and grandmother always told me to offer up my suffering to the Lord, because He had a reason for it.

My grandfather had a sister who came to America before him. She made it to Chicago and told him that if he came there, she could find him a good job. She offered to scrape some money together and mail it for a ticket.

It was the early 1900s, and many ocean liners brought countless immigrants from Europe to America, "the land of opportunity." They'd come to escape poverty, tyranny, and political unrest.

My grandfather heard there was a newly constructed ocean liner, built in Belfast, Northern Ireland. Upon departing from England it was to stop at Cohb, (Queenstown) Ireland with cheaper fares in third class at the bottom of the ship. He went to the mailbox every day, hoping for the money from his sister. Day after day, no money came.

Then the day arrived for the ship to leave for America. Feeling sad and dejected, Patrick felt he had missed his opportunity.

A number of days passed. Grandpa told me, "I heard a commotion around the newspaper stand. People were screaming and yelling, 'The *Titanic* sank, the *Titanic* sank." He looked straight at me and said, "You know, Kenny Michael, me boy [he often called me that], had I gotten on that ship, none of us would be here today." He ended by saying, "God works in strange and mysterious ways."

Then he would try to encourage me about my sufferings from polio. "I know it's not easy what you're going through, Kenny. But God has His divine ways of working things out for a good purpose. You may not see it now, but someday you will. Hang in there; don't give up."

My grandfather did see everything work out for the good. He was able to come to America on another ship. He was able to find another Irish immigrant to marry, and to raise a family of three children, my father being the youngest. He was able to see me, the second born of fifteen grandchildren.

Through my father and mother alone, who had nine children (including my late sister, Jean, who awaits us in heaven), there are thirty grandchildren (including our late son, Ryan) and two great-grandchildren. All because my grandfather believed God would work everything out.

The Bible refers to children as a gift and blessing from God: "Children are a heritage from the LORD, offspring a reward from him. Like arrows in the hands of a warrior are children born in one's youth. Blessed is the man whose quiver is full of them" (Psalm 127:3-5).

Suffering Helped Me Find the Gift of Music

When I became a teenager, I was fascinated by rock music and watched the Beatles on the *Ed Sullivan Show* in the early sixties. I had felt a rhythm deep in my soul and gravitated to the beat ever since zeroing in on the drums whenever I saw a marching band at a parade or a school band at a high school football game. My father took me to many of them, as he helped scout teams for his childhood buddy, who was a head coach at a local high school.

I would often get in trouble at the dinner table because I'd take a fork and knife and hit them on the plates, bowls, and cups. Eventually I graduated to a pair of bongos with chopsticks. Then, at thirteen years of age, I finally begged my father enough to buy me a set of drums.

I couldn't believe it when I sat behind a full set of drums. I could use both of my arms and hands well enough to play each drum and cymbal while my right foot could push the foot pedal on the bass drum. The only thing I could not move was the high hat because of a brace on my entire left leg. But many drummers just used the high-hat cymbals to ride on with one stick while the other hand hit the snare drum.

I amazed everyone with my ability to instantly play the drums, keep a steady beat, and even throw in timely rolls like any good drummer could. I found something I could do just as well as anyone who didn't have any physical challenges. I was on my way to playing the drums, singing, and organizing various bands for the next seven or eight years all over the Chicago area and two summers in Denver and Boulder, Colorado.

Music was about the only thing that helped me cope effectively throughout my teen years in high school. I needed something positive in my life during my early teen years, because I was unable to attend the local high school where my friends attended.

School authorities did not think the schools had the ability or the accommodations to handle students with physical challenges if there was a fire or an injury. There was no modern-day inclusion program or Americans with Disabilities Act for the rights of the disabled.

There was one high school in Chicago especially for teens and children with disabilities. It was called Spalding High School. I was picked up on the far south side of Chicago at 7:00 a.m. and returned home around 5:00 p.m. every day. Many buses picked up students all across Chicago and brought them to that school. As a whole I have many fond memories of my experience there.

Music still kept playing a big part in my life during my college years. I attended a local junior college in the area and continued playing music in a band. We were getting pretty good and went from performing at many local high schools for weekend "sock hops," as they were called, to playing at colleges and other venues.

One of my brothers, Steve, the second born, took up the guitar at my request when he was only twelve years old. He became an excellent guitarist at a very early age and performed with me for a number of years. A change in his path caused him to leave the band to complete his last year of high school near our home.

I continued to audition various musicians to keep a band going, even though it wasn't the same without my brother. I kept working with my music career but my heart wasn't in it.

As cool as I believed performing music was, I came to a place in my life where the song in my heart became dimmer. Even though at age twenty I had decided to stop attending college to pursue a music career, the right blend of band members wasn't working out.

Deep down I had a gnawing feeling that surely there was more to life. My limited understanding of the Bible at this time allowed me to have enough faith to believe there was a God. Even though I was not in the habit of reading or studying the Bible I accepted it was true and could be trusted. Still, I was searching for more.

Reflecting on my past, I see that I came to the biggest fork in the road. I had no idea God was leading me toward a "life-changing experience."

CHAPTER 8

A Life-Changing Experience

My parents did not have a lot when they were raising nine children. Mom worked constantly to run the daily household operations, which were insurmountable with getting everyone up and out the door on time for school, sporting events, jobs like paper routes, caddying at the local golf course, Cub Scouts, Boy Scouts, Girl Scouts, and so on.

Because of the great time pressures, my parents agreed it would be money well spent to hire a cleaning woman. She was a Polish immigrant who was very kind and caring. She had an unusually unique relationship with God and spoke freely about her faith in Christ.

Strangely, she seemed particularly drawn to speaking to me about her religious faith, the Bible, and Jesus Christ. She told me her life was changed after reading the Bible. I thought only trained clergy were allowed to actually read the Bible.

This maid spoke with me often about faith in God and said that He loved me and cared about me. Well, I had no problem with that, seeing that I was raised in an Irish Roman Catholic family on Chicago's South Side. I attended grade school at our local parish and went to Mass every week.

Suffering Led to a Spiritual Quest

Some of the things she said to me were new. She believed anyone could know for sure that they were going to heaven when they died. She often mentioned the term *born again.* According to her, a person would become "born again" and receive the assurance of eternal life if they prayed and asked Jesus Christ to forgive their sins and come into their life as Lord and Savior.

At that same time I was encountering many people who talked to me about their newfound relationship with Jesus. Local musician friends stopped over to my home and said they were attending a Bible study in the evenings and invited me to attend with them.

I paid a visit to the junior college I had attended to see some friends. While there, a student came up to me and said, "Didn't we meet at a concert where your band performed a while back?" He had been handing out invitations to a Tuesday evening Bible study at his home called the "Jesus Rap."

I thought, *Wait a minute, what's going on here? Why am I meeting all these individuals who are talking to me about Jesus Christ?* There were too many coincidences happening. It appeared there was a concerted effort by God to get my attention.

I decided to attend the next Tuesday evening Jesus Rap. There was a problem, though. When I'd ask a friend or two to attend with me, no one wanted to go. I would rarely go somewhere without a friend who could help me out of a chair or climb stairs.

Yet here I had to go solo. There was extra incentive because the cleaning lady told me Satan never wants you to attend any church or Bible study to hear the truth about Jesus, so he'll try to stop you every time. Well, I wasn't going to let that happen.

I arrived at the home where the Jesus Rap took place. I pulled up a little early and saw four or five stairs to get into the house. I could not climb them without help. Determined, I walked up to the house and immediately saw a kind-looking man who identified himself as the father of the student who invited me to his home.

He welcomed me and asked if I needed any assistance. I told him, "Yes, I need help to climb the stairs." I asked him, after I put my right foot on the stair, to pull me up each one by grabbing my right arm. Each step, he followed the order exactly. I got into the living room and thought, *Boy, I'm glad that's over.*

Then I heard the dreaded words, "The Bible study is in the basement." *Oh no*, I thought, *not the basement, my least favorite part of the house.* Well, the best way for me to get to the basement was to sit down on the floor and slide my butt down each and every step, one at a time. I thought, *How embarrassing,* as people heard *kerplunk, kerplunk*. I'm sure they were wondering what was happening. I made my grand entrance in a very public manner.

Suffering Led to a Personal Relationship with Christ

Embarrassed as I was, the people were extremely friendly and passionate about the Bible. Many talked about how close they felt to God, and they were excited about studying the Bible.

A number of individuals played guitars, and there were a few tambourines as they sang upbeat religious songs. For some reason I felt comfortable and hopeful that maybe God could change my life too.

At the conclusion of the meeting, one of the leaders asked everyone to bow their heads and close their eyes. He said, "If you'd like to know for sure you are going to heaven, you need to receive Jesus Christ as your Lord and Savior. Raise your hand now and I'll pray for you."

My heart began to beat faster, when all of a sudden I lifted my hand. Then the leader said, "If you raised your hand, repeat this prayer after me and say, 'Lord Jesus, come into my heart and forgive me of any sins. I believe You rose from the dead and surrender my life to You, and I confess You to be my Lord and Savior.'"

I was shown a passage of the Bible from Romans 10:9-10: "If you declare with your mouth, 'Jesus is Lord' and believe in your heart that God raised him from the dead, you will be saved. For it is with your heart that you believe and are justified, and it is with your mouth that you profess your faith and are saved."

This verse seemed to confirm clearly what I was being told. I received a deep peace and assurance in my being that something spiritually was awakening in the core of my life. I sensed God's presence in a way I never had before.

Granted, I had believed in God my whole life. I loved Jesus Christ to the best of my knowledge. But something was different here. My mind opened up to see biblical truths more clearly. I was not afraid to read the Bible on my own, but now I couldn't wait to start reading it. In fact, the cleaning woman had given me my own Bible just before I attended this Bible study.

I began to believe God had a purpose for my life. I felt my handicap from polio was easier to accept and

Ken Dignan

that the Lord wanted to use my suffering to show His strength, mercy, and grace. I was on my way to a unique and exciting lifestyle that would keep God as my central focus.

I came across another verse that day from Matthew 6:33: "Seek the Kingdom of God above all else, and live righteously, and he will give you everything you need" (NLT).

As strange as it may seem, my whole life went in a new and different direction. I was like a sponge, absorbing truths from the Bible every day.

I began reading the Bible often, if not every day. I attended the Jesus Rap every week and started to associate with many of the young adults my own age and with similar backgrounds.

I had stumbled onto, with God's help, the "Jesus Movement" of the early 70's and its loving participants, "the hippies." Long hair and t-shirts, blue jeans and beards, peasant dresses and headbands abounded. I fit right in. Music was a big part of our lives too, with guitar-led choruses permeating every gathering.

I became active at the church that sponsored the Jesus Rap. There was a lot of inspiring singing and helpful sermons from the Bible that could go thirty to forty-five minutes long. But I loved being exposed to the

Scriptures and followed right along in my Bible and took notes.

I learned what it meant to be *born again.* The term simply comes from the Gospel of John, where it says, "Jesus replied, 'Very truly I tell you, no one can see the kingdom of God unless they are born again.'"

"'How can someone be born when they are old?' Nicodemus asked. 'Surely they cannot enter a second time into their mother's womb to be born!' Jesus answered, 'Very truly I tell you, no one can enter the kingdom of God unless they are born of water and the Spirit. Flesh gives birth to flesh, but the Spirit gives birth to spirit. You should not be surprised at my saying, "You must be born again"' (John 3:3-7).

When you enter this world, you experience life as an infant and grow into childhood. In that process you develop mentally, emotionally, and physically. What about spiritual development?

Some would have you believe that this life is all there is. They believe that there is no God, no afterlife, nothing spiritual at all. But others sense a longing deep down inside where the soul resides. This separates humankind from the animal kingdom. There is something unique and different about human beings that cause them to reach out to God and spiritual things.

This is where a man or woman reaches out to Jesus Christ and God's spiritual world, for a new birth, and becomes "born again."

I plainly came to see that the Bible taught that one could know for sure they were going to heaven when they died. Until then, my religious training had not enlightened me to this truth. I believed in God and went to church all my life as a child and teenager. Now as a young adult twenty years of age, I came to receive Christ as my personal Lord and Savior.

I saw that God wanted all His children to live a life surrendered to Him. Having a daily, personal relationship with Jesus Christ was not only for priests, pastors, or people singled out in piety for vocational service. Every child of God was allowed and expected to live a vibrant life of faith each and every day.

I had a phenomenal change in my life for the good. I was more fulfilled and able to see things from God's perspective. I could accept my disability and deformity in a much better way.

Discovered a Passion to Teach the Bible

On Saturday evenings, I still attended the church where I grew up. On Sunday's I worshipped at the new church. I asked one of the priests if I could start a Bible study there for all the similar young people. I told him I had a burden to help people get a closer walk with the Lord and stay away from drugs, alcohol, and sex outside of marriage.

The priest asked me if I was attending preparatory seminary school, studying to become a priest. I told him no, not really, though it was a good thing—just not for me at that time. Then he told me, "I'm sorry, you can't teach a Bible study here unless you're studying for the priesthood." I felt bad about that, but what else could I do? I thanked him for his time.

Shortly thereafter, the new church I was attending had a couple of adult youth sponsors who said to me, "We've seen you attending here regularly and heard you share at some of the 'Jesus Raps.' We want to start another one and wondered if you'd like to lead and teach it."

It didn't take me too long to think about it. I said, "Sure, I'd be happy to." It started a few weeks later at someone else's home in the, you guessed it, basement.

I was well on my way toward deepening my understanding of the Bible and growing in the gifts of teaching the Scriptures. In fact, the senior pastor eventually started a class for adults before the service at what was called the Sunday school or school of the Bible.

Ken Dignan

The pastor invited me to team-teach the class with him. I came to class with my long hair and blue jeans, and he taught wearing a suit. There was always a lively discussion about the great doctrines of the Bible. The class kept growing, and many of us became stronger followers of Christ.

I was becoming a permanent fixture at the church. The senior pastor asked me if I needed a job. I told him yes. He told me that as he was praying for ways to use his time wisely, he got the idea to have me drive him to all his meetings, appointments, and hospital calls. He could prepare sermons, talk into a Dictaphone, and type by placing the typewriter on his briefcase, which lay on his lap.

My life was busily absorbed with developing new friendships, sharing my faith with others, helping to lead open souls to find Christ as their Savior, and teaching the Scriptures.

Attended College for Theological Training

The next best thing I could think of was to attend a Christian college and major in Bible and theology. I chose a college in the Minneapolis area called North Central Bible College. (Today, NCBC is called, North Central University.)

My handicap didn't slow me down at this time. I drove a car and could get in and out of it on my own. I could walk to classes from my dorm room. There were elevators throughout the college, which was one good reason I chose it. A number of friends from my new church, about twenty-six in all, attended there too. Many of the guys helped me in the dorm with getting dressed and showered, and assisted with toiletries. I was truly blessed.

My aptitude and thirst for learning the Bible and other subjects required in the liberal arts, such as English, science, math, and history, went well. I was getting top grades and really liked the whole college scene there.

After the conclusion of my first semester at NCBC I felt great about the direction in which I was heading. That summer I stayed active at my new church and spent quality time with my family.

I had a burden to help my whole family develop their relationship with Jesus. My brother Steve, who played the guitar in the bands, became a committed Christian along with me. He attended the Bible College, roomed with me and was part of the group that gave me assistance. But he felt led to go in a different direction college-wise, after his first semester.

After a long hot summer, which was refreshing and holiday-like, I couldn't wait to get back to college and continue to study. I was truly primed and pumped to dig into all my classes, especially the Bible and theology ones, which I could zero in on. I had already covered many of my general education courses required for my degree by attending two semesters in the local junior college upon graduating from high school; they all transferred.

A Special Honor to Preach

That Christmas I went home during the holiday break. I was chosen as one of three Bible College students to preach combined mini-sermons on the same topic during the Sunday evening service between Christmas and New Year's.

I was honored to be asked to share the pulpit, like a regular minister. I invited my parents to attend. They rarely visited a worship service at a church other than a Roman Catholic one. I was happy they agreed to come.

Everything went well, and my parents appeared open to what they heard. My dad and mom said they were proud of me. They could see I was following a calling that looked past my handicap and my denominational upbringing, as God was preparing to use me for His glory.

A Family Crisis Led to
a Gut-Wrenching Suffering

I couldn't have imagined what twists and turns the next few days held in store for me and my family. I went back to college the weekend after the holidays, settled back into dorm life, and went to church the next day, Sunday.

When I got back to my dorm room, I heard the public phone ringing down the hall. Whoever answered it usually called out who it was for. I heard, "Ken, phone call for you." I thought, *Who's calling me at this time of the day?*

I went to the phone and heard my father's voice. He was crying. I heard others in the background crying too. My father said, "Ken, Jeanie's dead. Jeanie died." My heart started pounding out of my chest. Jean was the fourth sibling, the first girl after three boys. Surely I hadn't heard that right. I said, "What, Dad? What did you say?"

He said, "There were car problems, and your sister passed away." It was one of those surreal moments when you feel as if you are in a dream, when you even hope it is a dream. My father said he would help me get home quicker by purchasing an airplane ticket. My last words to him were, "I'll get home as soon as I can."

I had never flown in a commercial airliner before and didn't like traveling by myself because of my disability. Knowing I had to get home quickly, I cast aside any worries about flying and headed for the airport.

I had a credit card from my father for emergencies, so my friends drove me to the Minneapolis-St. Paul airport and I purchased the ticket. It seemed like everything was going in slow motion. All I could think of was getting home ASAP.

The plane took off, and I prayed all the way for God to give me wisdom. What could I say to my family? How could I answer the questions like, Why did God allow this to happen? Why didn't God spare us this tragedy by allowing Jeanie to live a long and normal life?

While 30,000 feet in the air, I believed God was speaking to my heart. I sensed in my thoughts, *He has a plan we cannot see yet. He can turn bad, negative things into something good if we'll trust Him and turn it over to Him and His will.*

That thought gave me peace. The plane landed at Midway airport and I joined my family. I remember sitting with everyone in the small living room of our bungalow that housed eleven people, now ten.

My mom and dad, brothers and sisters were all crying and hugging each other. I prayed for supernatural strength and calm. Then I said, "Let me share with all of you a thought I believe the Lord gave to me. We may never really know in this life why Jeanie had to die at only seventeen years of age. But if we'll trust in God and ask Jesus to help us, something good can come out of this for our whole family."

I read from the same Bible verse I'd lean on time and again that would comfort me from Romans 8:28: "And we know that in all things God works for the good of those who love him, who have been called according to his purpose." This is a recurring theme and verse in this book.

My dad asked me to say a prayer for our family. I asked God to comfort all of us and give us peace, strength, mercy, and grace, so we could all make it through this terrible trial.

Later that evening, I asked my mother if she wanted to ask Jesus Christ to be her Savior and Lord. She said yes. I was sitting at the kitchen table and my mom knelt down right there and leaned over the table. I asked her to say the same prayer I had prayed a few years earlier.

I said, "Mom, say this prayer and repeat it after me: 'Lord Jesus, come into my heart and forgive me of any sins. I believe You rose from the dead and I surrender my life to You. I confess You to be my Lord and Savior.

I believe You rose from the dead and desire to give me the gift of eternal life.'" Tears were flowing from our eyes as we hugged each other.

The Funeral

Those next few days were rough. I remember our family standing in line by Jean's casket in a row according to our ages; I was the oldest and stood next to Mom. It was freezing cold that second week of January. Countless people came to the funeral home.

There were hundreds of girls from Jean's high school, Mount Assisi in Lemont, Illinois. At times, we were told, the line to get in stretched outside for many blocks. I never saw so many people crying in one place for an extended period of time.

I was very much drained the night of the wake. Then we had the funeral service and burial at the cemetery. I thanked God for a deep peace I had that Jeanie was in heaven with the Lord Jesus.

The Accident

I had taken Jean to a Bible study and talked to her a number of times about receiving Christ as her Savior. I was certain she was open to Christ as her Savior and at peace with God. We all took great comfort in that.

My father and mother told me the story of how my sister died. Apparently, her boyfriend's mother noticed that her automobile needed a new muffler. She took it to a repair shop, and a new one was installed.

On her way home, she noticed a slight headache and sick feeling. She wondered if the muffler had been installed properly, so she kept her windows cracked open to allow fresh air into the car.

Her son wanted to borrow the car so he and Jeanie could go out for the evening. His mother hesitated but finally gave in, because he promised he'd be sure to keep the windows open too.

They parked the car on a side street in the area, and my sister and her boyfriend were inside with the car running to keep warm. Neighbors saw the car running and what looked like smoke coming out of the engine.

They called the fire department, which arrived with an ambulance only to find my sister and her boyfriend passed out inside. They endeavored to revive them on the spot but quickly rushed the young people to the hospital.

My sister never regained consciousness, and the doctors concluded she died from carbon monoxide poisoning. Her boyfriend responded to treatments and gained consciousness and lived.

Authorities concluded they did not leave enough airflow from open windows to expel enough of the odorless carbon monoxide fumes. The investigation concluded there was no foul play or attempted suicide but that it was a terrible accident caused by a botched mechanical job (1).

Something Positive Came Immediately

My parents and family were very upset about all this, and when the boyfriend was released from the hospital, they wanted to go to his home to talk to him and his parents. My mother asked me if I'd go along, and I did not hesitate and nodded my head yes.

When we went into the home, everyone's eyes were moist from tears. Here was a young man who had just lost his girlfriend, and his parents, who felt terrible about allowing their son to take the car out that fateful evening.

My father was angry at times, and rightly so; I could see that. There was a Scripture I felt spoke about the best way to react. I shared it with my father before we left. It is found in Romans 12:17-21:

> Do not repay anyone evil for evil. Be careful to do what is right in the eyes of everyone. If it is possible, as far as it depends on you, live at peace with everyone. Do not take revenge, my dear

friends, but leave room for God's wrath,
for it is written: "It is mine to avenge; I
will repay," says the Lord. On the contrary:
"If your enemy is hungry, feed him; if he
is thirsty, give him something to drink. In
doing this, you will heap burning coals on
his head."' Do not be overcome by evil,
but overcome evil with good.

I prayed for God to heal every hurting heart and give His divine peace to everyone in the room. My parents asked questions, talked, and got things off their chests, as did my sister's boyfriend's parents and the boyfriend. Basically everyone was so sorry it had happened. It was a terrible accident no one ever expected.

The time came for us to leave after more tears and disbelief that this accident had actually occurred. As we left the home of my sister's boyfriend, I could see my dad was beginning to lay aside his anger. I kept praying inside my heart for continued miracles of taking negative situations and turning them into something positive for God's glory.

Another Miracle of Transformation

On the way home, we had to drive by the Stone Church. The parking lot was packed, and my mother asked, "What's going on at your church, Ken?"

I told her there was a prayer service each night that week to help bless and lead the ministries for the New Year. My mom said to my father, "Lee, can we stop and attend the service?" My father didn't seem too thrilled about seeing more people after what he'd just gone through at the boyfriend's home. To my surprise he said, "All right, Rosemary, I'll turn in."

We parked and went in to the service, which was already in progress. It was toward the end, and the preaching had concluded, as had the singing and prayers.

Finally the senior pastor, my dear friend, The Rev. Owen Carr, who mentored me, allowed me to teach classes with him, and gave me a job being his chauffer, asked, "Does anyone else have any other needs or burdens on their heart for us to lift in prayer?"

Out of nowhere my father stood up. Now, he was a private man who kept most things to himself. For him to stand up in a church he'd attended only once, a week or so before, to hear me preach, was a miracle.

My father said, "I wanted to thank many of you who came to the wake for my seventeen-year-old daughter, who passed away last week. I also wish to thank you for reaching out to my son Ken, in whom we've seen such marvelous changes since he started coming here and gave his life to Christ."

Then the pastor asked my father if he wanted to come forward for prayer to surrender his life to Christ, and he said yes. To my amazement, he walked down the aisle to make a public profession of his faith in Christ. He knelt down in the front of the auditorium with the pastor and numerous others who came to pray with him.

I was seeing miracles take place already, not long after my dear sister Jean passed on to heaven. I was able to see both my father and mother surrender their lives wholly to God. They began a deeper commitment to put God first in everything they did and to grow in their personal relationship with Jesus.

I called the college and explained to them the situation and shared my desire to spend the rest of the month at home with my family, helping to be a support.

The college took the month of January to offer students the opportunity to take one class during what was called the Jan. Term. I withdrew from that course and stayed home.

I was very thankful to have been used by God to encourage and care for my whole family and offer them Christ-like, biblical-type love. We prayed many prayers that month, and my whole family began to attend occasional Sunday services at the new church I was involved with.

As time went on, my parents became very active at the new church, and years later, my father was even elected to serve on the board of deacons for many years. A number of my siblings kept attending the new church, and some went back to attending the church we grew up in.

It is clear that God can take tough situations and use them to bring people closer to Him. He definitely uses suffering to get our attention so we will hold on to Him for dear life. Difficulties can cause us to jump into our heavenly Father's arms much in the same way children wrap their arms around their parents and squeeze them, not wanting to let go when being dropped off with a babysitter.

In heaven there will not be any denominational labels. There's no section for Roman Catholics, Greek Orthodox, Anglicans, Lutherans, Baptists, Pentecostals, and so on. Heaven will be filled with individuals who received Jesus Christ as their Savior and Lord and accepted God's gift of salvation as given by grace. Grace means "unmerited favor." You can't earn it or deserve it.

"For it is by grace you have been saved, through faith— and this is not from yourselves, it is the gift of God— not by works, so that no one can boast" (Ephesians 2:8-10).

Max Lucado put it like this:

The words of "Amazing Grace" are yours. Though written around 1773, they bring hope like today's sunrise. "'Tis grace hath brought me safe thus far, and grace will lead me home." You have his Spirit within you. Heavenly hosts above you. Jesus Christ interceding for you. You have God's sufficient grace to sustain you. Paul's life underscored this truth. He wrote, "There was given me a thorn in my flesh, a messenger of Satan, to torment me. Three times I pleaded with the Lord to take it away from me. But he said to me, 'My grace is sufficient for you, for my power is made perfect in weakness'" (2 Cor. 12:9).

A thorn in the flesh. Such vivid imagery. The sharp end of a thorn pierces the soft skin of life and lodges beneath the surface. Every step is a reminder of the thorn in the flesh. The cancer in the body. The sorrow in the heart. The child in the rehab center. The red ink on the ledger. The felony on the record. The craving for whiskey in the middle of the day. The tears in the middle of the night. The thorn in the flesh. "Take it away," you've pleaded. Not once, twice, or even three times. You've out-prayed Paul.

He prayed a sprint; you've prayed the Boston Marathon. And you're about to hit the wall at mile nineteen. The wound radiates pain, and you see no sign of tweezers coming from heaven. But what you hear is this: "My grace is sufficient for you." (2)

A life-changing experience taught me to be thankful for gaining a clear, meaningful knowledge of the Bible. The Scriptures hold all the keys to knowing who we are, where we came from, where we are going, and how to get there.

The Bible is the most important book in the entire world. When you look at it openly and honestly, from a theological and scholarly standpoint, you will understand all the great mysteries of life. Ultimately you come to know the almighty God. In so doing you will come to know "the author of life" (Hebrews 12:2).

An essential element of knowing God and His word is recognizing the importance of suffering in a believer's life. I can earnestly encourage you and say, "Don't waste your suffering."

CHAPTER 9

Don't Waste Your Suffering

A s a minister, preacher, and theologian I knew what the Bible taught about suffering: Suffering has a place in everyone's life. It is a mystery why some suffer more than others. It's a mystery why God allows some very good and godly people to suffer more than some non-Christian, selfish, hurtful individuals.

God doesn't want us to waste our sorrows from suffering. The Christian life is filled with many challenges. One of the toughest ones is dealing with and providing answers to the question of this book: Why does Jesus allow suffering?

One of the shortest verses in the Bible, John 11:35, says, "Jesus wept." Three times in this passage Jesus shows his anger at illness and suffering. Jesus addresses the reasons for suffering, maybe not directly or specifically but indirectly, by pointing out His own willingness to suffer and by displaying how suffering gives God the Father an opportunity to show His strength and comfort to those being refined by its process.

Faulty Reasoning

Jesus Christ answered the question that has been on the minds of people since the beginning of time: *When something bad happens to you, isn't it because you or someone close to you did something bad, sinful, or wrong?* A number of biblical principles must be considered in determining how to know whether or not a trial is sent by God.

God has set the world in motion with gravity, atmospheric pressure, earthquakes, tornados, airplane or automobile crashes, dangerous choices people make with drunk or reckless driving, and a host of other things that occur. God can intervene or choose not to, it's up to Him.

Numerous theologians do not believe God spends all of His time, as if humans are marionettes on His strings dropped from heaven, saying who experiences a tragedy and who doesn't. What is sure to me is that God is sovereign, which means He can do whatever He wants to. But whether or not He specifically sends every single tragedy, accident, or trial is often a divine mystery. It's best to trust God in the midst of the hard times or tragedies and commit your life to Him realizing He'll work everything out according to His purpose and plan.

In Job's case, Satan sent the enemies, the fire, and the storms that stole his cattle and burned his crops and fields, along with causing all his children, their spouses and his grandchildren to die.

On the other hand, God intervened to stop a lion from killing Daniel, a famine from starving Elijah to death, a prison from holding Peter for long, and a crowd from killing Paul. God's interventions, plans, and purposes for each life, when it comes to suffering, will vary. I believe we will never be able to figure out why or how God decides the plan for each individual's life in this world.

How God can personally know, love, and intervene in the lives of billions and billions of people at one time is beyond our capability to understand and even grasp. We will have to leave it in God's hands until we get to heaven, where, with a new mind and new way of thinking, we can accept and receive all the reasoning of the Almighty God.

Learning About Suffering, Prayer, and Divine Healing

Early in my walk with Christ a number of Christians, though well meaning, began to tell me that it was God's will to miraculously heal me from my disability—that all my physical problems, muscle weaknesses, and deformities could disappear like in the times Jesus walked the earth.

Some told me it wasn't God's will for me to be handicapped. They said God wanted me to confess my healing, believe without any doubt, and act in faith as if I had the miracle before I actually saw it. "That's faith," I was taught.

I had a weak and deformed left leg and relied on a steel brace attached by leather straps. The brace extended the length of my whole leg, foot to hip. After a number of times numerous friends at church prayed, they told me I should take off my brace and walk before I got healed. That would show I had the right kind of faith to be healed.

I felt—well, I know—God can heal and that with faith anything can happen, so I took off the brace and walked. I could always walk without the brace even though that leg was very thin, the muscles were atrophied, and my knee could buckle easily and give out.

I was filled with joy about my newfound faith in Christ. I was consumed with studying the Bible and attending church services and Bible teaching classes. Now here I was walking carefully and cautiously, hoping I wouldn't fall.

I told people God had healed me, and in all sincerity I knew God could do it, while I hoped every step of the way that He *would* do it. Two or three days passed, and I didn't notice any difference.

Then that next Sunday evening, after coming home from the worship service, I came into the house at the back kitchen door. I took a few steps, and out of nowhere, my left leg buckled and gave out. It bent, and all my weight collapsed on it as the leg got twisted underneath my back.

I felt a big "snap, crackle and pop." My family and friends came to my aid and pulled my leg out from underneath me. It was throbbing and very painful. It began to swell below my knee as if I'd swallowed a football and it had gotten stuck there.

The following morning we went to the hospital for X-rays, which revealed that the leg was broken and would have to be casted. It would take two or three months to heal.

Now what would I do? I felt like I had failed God because I didn't have enough faith. I was greatly embarrassed. I had told my family and other people I was healed with the hope that they would give their lives to Christ as Savior and Lord.

Besides this, I was in a lot of pain and discomfort, and was greatly hindered in my already limited mobility. My faith and trust in God was being tested. It was a bit shaken but not depleted.

In fact, God used it to build my understanding of prayer, faith, and divine healing. It was obviously paramount for me to gain a broad understanding of how suffering and illness correlated with faith, prayer for the sick and divine healing. It would definitely become a passion of mine to help others deal with what the Bible teaches about this. In fact, the topic of divine healing became the theme and research of my first book. It was titled *'Til Healing Comes.*

Suffering Can Lead You to Pray for a Healing

You can't read the Bible without seeing that God can and does heal His children miraculously. Early on, in the Jewish Old Testament Scriptures, you see a statement about who God is: Exodus 15:26, "I am the Lord who heals you." In the Hebrew, the language of the Old Testament, this phrase is translated as "Jehovah Rapha," which means "The Lord our Healer."

The first time we see that God can heal through the prayers of His children is in Genesis 20:17, where it says, "Then Abraham prayed to God, and God healed Abimelek, his wife and his female slaves so they could have children again." Here it is revealed that God wants His followers to come before Him in prayer whenever they are sick or dealing with an illness.

In Exodus 23:25, God told His people the importance of worship and obedience to Him regarding healing. He said, "Worship the Lord your God, and his blessing will be on your food and water. I will take away sickness from among you."

In the New Testament we see that the early church practiced prayer for healing of the sick:

> Is anyone among you in trouble? Let them pray. Is anyone happy? Let them sing songs of praise. Is anyone among you sick? Let them call the elders of the church to pray over them and anoint them with oil in the name of the Lord. And the prayer offered in faith will make the sick person well; the Lord will raise them up. If they have sinned, they will be forgiven. Therefore confess your sins to each other and pray for each other so that you may be healed. The prayer of a righteous person is powerful and effective. (James 5:13-17)

God desires to have His children come before Him in prayer whenever they are sick. Miracles of divine healing can and do happen. They have occurred throughout the ages at different times and specific places

However, experience can reveal to us that healings occurred much more frequently during Bible times, especially with Jesus in the Gospels and the Book of Acts. Jesus used miracles to give credence to the validity of His ministry and message. Plus the miracles recorded in the four Gospels focused in on a three year period and a small geographical area confined to the cities surrounding Jerusalem.

Jesus did not grant a miracle of divine healing for every sick person in the Jerusalem area during His ministry. In John 5:1-9 at the pool of Bethesda many laid there once a year hoping for a miracle. The first one in the pool was healed after an angel of the Lord stirred the water. A man who couldn't walk or move laid there annually for 38 years. Jesus went up to him and he was healed. None of the other infirm people were healed at the pool that day. (1)

Therefore it is important to realize that no sure formula is given in Scripture to guarantee anyone that God will grant them a miracle. One must leave the results of their prayers to the Lord and His specific will.

Miracles come according to God's sovereign plan and purpose. Whereas suffering is a part of God's overall plan, one never knows exactly what particular details God wills for anyone's life. As a whole, whenever He performs a healing through prayer, it is to share only a foretaste and shadow of what is to come in the heavenly kingdom.

"And you also were included in Christ when you heard the message of truth, the gospel of your salvation.

When you believed, you were marked in him with a seal, the promised Holy Spirit, who is a deposit guaranteeing our inheritance until the redemption of those who are God's possession—to the praise of his glory" (Ephesians 1:13-14).

What the Holy Spirit works in the lives of all who believe is considered a deposit guaranteeing what is to come in Heaven. There have been and will be periodic miracles and blessings in this life. But they are only a small portion of all the blessings and benefits the children of God will receive in Heaven, where there will be no more pain, suffering, sorrow, tears, or grief, as you've seen in Revelation 21:4. This could be one of the theme verses used often in this book.

Balanced, Biblically Based Beliefs on Healing

A book of this nature on why God allows suffering may concentrate more on the positive aspects of how to handle suffering. Still by no means should anyone get the idea that it's not right to do everything within your abilities to alleviate your suffering through prayer, medicine, doctors, nutrition, exercise, or whatever else.

It's not wrong to come to the Lord whenever you are sick or suffering and ask Him to heal you. Though suffering is a big part of life on earth, one is always encouraged to follow the instructions of Scripture and ask God for a miraculous healing. The key is to commit your life to the Lord and leave the results of your need in His hands. Whether a miracle occurs or not, the best action is to trust and follow God no matter what.

I'm convinced that God's word teaches that healing is available at times according to His plan, purpose, and providence. That said, much of what is written, taught, and televised about miracles today goes beyond what the Bible says. What's needed is a sound, balanced, biblically based theology on divine healing, suffering, and miracles.

I like the lyrics to a song I heard by a contemporary Christian musical group called Kutless. It is a meaningful song about the topic of healing and suffering written by Tony Wood and Scott Krippayne, titled "Even If." (2)

The lyrics are as follows:

Sometimes all we have to hold on to
Is what we know is true of who You are
So when the heartache hits like a hurricane
That could never change who You are
And we trust in who You are

Even if the healing doesn't come
And life falls apart
And dreams are still undone
You are God You are good

Forever faithful One
Even if the healing
Even if the healing doesn't come

Lord we know your ways are not our ways
So we set our faith in who You are
Even though You reign high above us
You tenderly love us
We know Your heart
And we rest in who You are

You're still the Great and Mighty One
We trust You always
You're working all things for our good
We'll sing your praise

You are God and we will bless You
As the Good and Faithful One
You are God and we will bless You
Even if the healing doesn't come

God promises to Be with You in Suffering

Good, godly people will face all sorts of trouble, problems, and pain. But God has promised to be with them and to add comfort, peace, and strength. It's much like a young child being able to face a severe loud thunder and lightning storm if they're in bed with a father or mother. God will not keep you from trouble, but He will be with you in your trouble.

We see examples of this with God when He was with Joseph, one of the twelve sons of Jacob, as he was sold by his brothers into slavery and then imprisoned for a crime his didn't commit (Genesis 37-50); or with the disciples in the boat in the midst of a storm at sea (Mark 4:38-39); or with Paul and Silas at midnight in prison (Acts 16:25-26).

God does not say He will keep His children from experiencing any problems. What He does promise is to stand with them as they go through problems. We see this well documented in the following Scriptures:

"God is our refuge and strength, an ever-present help in trouble. Therefore we will not fear, though the earth gives way and the mountains fall into the heart of the sea, though its waters roar and foam and the mountains quake with their surging" (Psalm 46:1-3).

"When you pass through the waters, I will be with you; and when you pass through the rivers, they will not sweep over you. When you walk through the fire, you will not be burned; the flames will not set you ablaze" (Isaiah 43:2).

"'For I know the plans I have for you,' says the LORD. 'They are plans for good and not for disaster, to give you a future and a hope'" (Jeremiah 29:11 [NLT]).

If you realize God has promised to be with you in the midst of your suffering and pain, you can confidently take comfort in knowing that truth and receive emotional, physical, and spiritual relief. We see this elaborated from the words of the apostle Peter here: "May the God of all grace, who called us to His eternal glory by Christ Jesus, after you have suffered a while, perfect, establish, strengthen, and settle you" (1 Peter 5:10).

We must always keep in mind that whatever we go through any day, good or bad, Christ is there with us. He has promised to work all things together for our good. He has promised to use our trials to keep us humble and trusting in Him, to rid us little by little of our pride, ego, and selfishness, to use suffering to help us appreciate all He went through for us through His life, death, burial, and resurrection.

Suffering Is like the Birthing Process for God's Plans

Incidents of suffering in your life are not accidents. According to the Scriptures that speak about God's sovereignty, nothing in the life of a follower of Christ comes by accident. Whether good circumstances come into your life or bad, painful, hard times come, God is arranging your experiences for a reason. God uses tough times to push, prod, and prepare you to be conformed to His providence, purpose, and plan.

The birthing process is usually not without pain and discomfort. When God is trying to birth something in you, there will more than likely be some type of suffering involved. Suffering is like God's emergency broadcast system that He uses to get our attention. He says, "Let me interrupt this life for a test of our ..." Suffering often causes us to reflect, resolve, and redirect our steps.

That's why James could confidently say the following:

> Consider it pure joy, my brothers and sisters, whenever you face trials of many kinds, because you know that the testing of your faith produces perseverance. Let perseverance finish its work so that you may be mature and complete, not lacking anything. If any of you lacks wisdom, you should ask God, who gives generously to all without finding fault, and it will be given to you. (James 1:2-5)

This passage has baffled many who wonder why they should welcome their trials as friends. It is humanly difficult and experientially unrealistic for anyone, without God's help, to approach difficulties so positively. James unfolds the truth that their purpose is to test and strengthen our faith. He is saying our problems serve to develop our perseverance.

God is always endeavoring to teach us some spiritual truth to help us grow stronger and develop our Christian life. Christ wants us to be strong in faith and to trust Him to guide us and provide for our daily needs. In what is often called the Lord's Prayer, Jesus said to pray, "Give us this day our daily bread" (Matthew 6:11).

Notice He said "daily bread." Not enough to cover us for a few days, weeks, or months, but only for today. I tie this together with another Bible correlation in the Old Testament where God provided Moses and the children of Israel only enough Manna in the wilderness for each day (Exodus 16, John 6:39, 41, 58).

Suffering and pain can either draw you closer to God and faith or pull you further away and feed your doubts and questions about the existence of God and the truths of the Bible.

Suffering and the Holocaust

I read something recently to further illustrate this, from an online newsletter called *Church and Culture,* by James Emery White, whom I quoted earlier. The quote is rather long but effective. It is as follows:

> Holocaust survivor Elie Wiesel put the memory of the horrors of his experience to words in a book that was appropriately called *'Night.'* One of the nightmares he

describes has to do with the hanging of a young boy who was suspected of sabotage in a Nazi death camp by the German Gestapo.

They began by torturing the boy. When he would not confess, they sentenced him to death with two other prisoners, leading all three in chains to the gallows. It was to be a public execution, and thousands of prisoners were forced to watch.

While the head of the camp read the verdict, all eyes were on the child. His face was pale, and he was nervously biting his lips. No more than 12 years-old, Wiesel writes that he had the face of a sad angel. The three victims mounted the chairs, and their necks were placed within the nooses.

The child said nothing.

Suddenly, someone cried out, "Where is God? Where is He?"

No one answered.

The executioner then tipped the three chairs over so that the bodies fell, jerking to a stop at the end of the ropes. Though the crowd was large, not a sound was heard. The only movement was the setting of the sun on the horizon. The only noise was the sound of men weeping.

The two adults died instantly. Their tongues hung swollen, tinged with blue. But the third rope, the one holding the little boy, was still moving. For more than half-an-hour, he hung there, struggling between life and death, dying in slow agony under their eyes. Unfeeling and insolent, the guards ordered the prisoners to march past the two dead bodies, along with the still struggling boy.

As Wiesel passed, he writes that he could not help but turn and gaze into the boy's eyes. As he did, behind him, he heard the voice say again, "Where is God now?" And Wiesel said that the inner voice of his heart answered, "Where is He? Here He is—He is hanging here on this gallows."

For Elie Wiesel, that ended any chance of Him relating to God. For him, God died that day.

But God didn't "die" for everyone.

I read an interview of a man by the name of Christian Reger who spent four years as a prisoner at Dachau for nothing more than belonging to the Confessing Church, the branch of the German state church which opposed Hitler. Later he became a leader of the International Dachau Committee, and returned to the grounds in order to restore the camp as a monument so that the world would not forget.

In the interview, Reger reflected how the German philosopher Nietzsche said a man can undergo torture if he knows the *why* of his life. "But I, here at Dachau, learned something far greater. I learned to know the Who of my life. He was enough to sustain me then, and is enough to sustain me still."

Are you there yet? In the face of staggering questions and assaults against your faith, and even against God's character, are you content with the *Who* of your life as opposed to the often-empty nature of the *why*?

Throughout our faith journey we will experience doubt—doubt about the goodness of God, the wisdom of God, even the truth of God. Dachau moments,

Moments when you wonder what God is *really* like. Sometimes it can seem that the God of the Bible acts in ways that we would never dream of acting, which makes it hard to believe *that* God—or what we think we *know* about that God—is *right*; much less that He is worthy of worship and obedience.

For what it's worth, such moments are normal. They are simply moments of questions, of doubt, of facing the mystery of God in light of the reality of our broken world. It's what you *do* with them that matters.

Of course, much that we lay at God's feet belongs at our own. Much of the evil and suffering and insanity of this world is self-inflicted. Dachau itself was a reflection of human depravity, and was meant to be as evil as it was. Even the first camp commandant, an SS officer named Theodor Eicke, had been plucked from a psychiatric hospital due to his sanity being questioned by the local Nazi leadership.

Fitting, in a way, as Dachau was insanity made manifest. But it was human insanity, not God's. (3)

195

Tragic Suffering Can Manifest
Human Uniqueness

The Holocaust definitely is a terrible blight on mankind in the history of unconscionable suffering. To exterminate millions of Jewish lives proves that man, apart from God, is a sinful, potentially wicked lot.

The tragedy of the December 26, 2004, tsunami on Sri Lanka, India, and Thailand, where more than 230,000 lives perished, speaks volumes to a broken and suffering world. Remarkably, in the midst of that, a family of five was vacationing in that region for Christmas break. They were in a resort swimming pool when the tsunami struck with a vengeance.

All of a sudden the father, Henry Belon, mother, Maria, and their sons, ages fourteen, seven, and five, were separated. Miraculously the mother survived the rushing ocean waters and found her fourteen-year-old son. The father survived and found their seven- and five-year-old sons. Eventually, through a host of miraculous events, this separated family became reunited and survived bodily harm.

This story is documented to zero in on just one among many survivors, with a movie titled *The Impossible.* I share this to show that in the midst of horrific suffering and tragedy, strange and mysterious things happen.

I believe God created human beings in His image. This image does not mean we look like God outwardly but it is revealed by inner qualities. Humans have a unique gamut of emotions they can show. They have sheer determination to persist and survive under insurmountable odds.

God can and does perform miracles of survival in the lives of many during catastrophes and tragedies. Whereas on the other hand, numerous souls perish and face eternity. This exhibits God's providence and sovereignty beyond our ability to figure out.

On December 14, 2012, in New Town, Connecticut, a troubled twenty-year-old man entered Sandy Hook Elementary School, shooting and killing twenty six- and seven-year-old children and six staff members as well as wounding two others. Earlier that morning at home he had shot his mother, killing her. When authorities arrived, the young shooter turned a gun on himself and he died.

This chilling event captivated America and the world with another terrible tragedy causing untold grief, suffering, and pain. Again we heard, "Where was God?"

I heard a Christian news commentator by the name of Mike Huckabee on the Fox News network address that question. "After the [Sandy Hook School] tragedy, God did show up in the teachers who sacrificed themselves to save their students, the hugs and tears of family members, the policemen who risked their lives, in the church vigils, and in the White House, where the president invoked His name and quoted from His book." (4)

I watched the national broadcast of the area-wide interfaith service where many of the victims' families were in attendance, along with numerous first responders and local clergy. You could witness healing hugs, tears, prayers, and words of Scripture and thoughts about grief and suffering.

Learning Lessons from Many Falls

In the midst of adversity you may feel like you've been knocked off your feet. Trouble can knock you down and knock you out. When you feel that way, you need to remain strong in faith even though tough times can cause you to feel you can't make it.

A passage in 2 Corinthians 4:1-12 has meant a lot to me:

> This priceless treasure we hold, so to speak, in a common earthenware jar— to show that the splendid power of it belongs to God and not to us. We are handicapped on all sides, but we are never frustrated; we are puzzled, but

> never in despair. We are persecuted,
> but we never have to stand it alone: we
> may be knocked down but we are never
> knocked out! Every day we experience
> something of the death of the Lord Jesus,
> so that we may also know the power of
> the life of Jesus in these bodies of ours.
> (J. B. Phillips Translation)

I have frequently been literally knocked down because of poor balance from my disability. If I fell, I couldn't get up by myself. I've been dependent on others every day of my life. It's humbling, challenging, and embarrassing to fall and be unable to get up off the ground. It is also dangerous, and I've suffered numerous concussions and contusions often requiring stitches.

I've learned many life lessons from all the times I've fallen. What amazed me was that I'd get up every time and keep going forward with my head held high. Throughout my life my ability to balance myself when standing was very poor. The slightest wrong move could knock me off my feet.

It often embarrassed me to fall as a child outside my home. If I was playing on our front lawn or near the sidewalk and fell, I'd have to wait until my mother, a family member, or a neighbor either looked out the window or came outside and saw me on the ground and helped me up.

If a stranger walked by, I'd often pretend I was playing with something on the ground, fearing they might ask if I needed any assistance. Usually when they asked, I'd say, "No, I'm just playing out here."

I fell numerous times playing at the playground or tripping on a curb or concrete step. My head frequently hit the ground so hard, it would split open, requiring a trip to the hospital for stitches. Occasionally my head hit the ground so hard, I experienced concussion-like symptoms.

I can remember a number of times I took some tough falls when I got older:

Once I went to a gym near the church where I was a youth pastor, so I could meet our young men's church league basketball team and coach their practice. My love for sports came from having five brothers and a father who were all very athletic. Not being able to play sports led me to do a lot of basketball and baseball coaching through the years. I called myself "a student of the games."

The practice was in late October, and it was darker by early evening. I got out of my car and slipped on some rocks, which caused me to fall. It was dark, there was no one around, and I wondered how I'd get help.

Suddenly, I saw a young boy coming down the street riding his bicycle. As he came near me, I called out to him. "Hey, stop, I need some help. I'm handicapped, and I've fallen and can't get up. There are some guys in the gym, and if you'll go in there, tell them their pastor fell and needs help."

He replied, "How do I know you're not going to hurt me?" I said, "Don't leave. Look, here's my deformed right arm." I waved it at him so he could see it. I went on, "I'm not lying. Seriously, please help me." Finally, he said, "Okay."

He ran into the gym and told the guys, and they all came running out. A couple of them rolled me over and pulled me to my feet. After gaining my balance, I thanked them and the kid for helping me. I went on to coach the practice, having survived another fall.

Then there was the time when I was in seminary. Of course I was able to walk back then, though not for long distances. I lived only a block and a half away. That allowed me to walk there.

One day as I was walking to the seminary, I twisted my ankle on the curb and lost my balance, which caused me to crash to the ground. It was around 8:00 a.m. I had a few drivers honk at me and say something like, "You derelict, go home and sleep it off."

Not one driver stopped to see if I was hurt or needed help. Finally, someone walked by and I was able to explain my situation. That person helped me get to my feet so I could carry on my schedule for the day. I was glad God gave me a thick hide and a strong will not to let bumps in the road keep me from going forward.

I could write a whole chapter on all my falls. Suffice it to say that a few others stand out. I was the host of a contemporary Christian radio program every Monday from 7:00 p.m. to 10:00 p.m. on a station not far from the St. Louis, Missouri, area. I was an associate pastor in Jerseyville, Illinois, which was around forty-five minutes away.

The station was a little way outside of town. It was a winter evening, and when I got out of the car, I slipped on some ice and fell. I was close enough to my car to crawl to the front seat, as the door was still open. There was a CB radio in my car; it was the early eighties, before cell phones.

People used CB radios a lot out there to communicate with more than truck drivers. My handle was Joyful Noise. I got to my radio and was able to reach the microphone to call out, "Breaker Nineteen, this is Joyful Noise. Anyone out there?" After a few tries, someone responded, so I said, "This is Joyful Noise, Pastor Ken.

I've fallen outside the WJBM radio station. Can you call the person in the station and tell them I fell in the parking lot and need help?"

They called the station and spoke to the DJ I was to relieve. He put on a song and ran out to help me. I was quite cold and shook up a bit but able to compose myself to get on the air at 7:00 p.m. sharp and say, "This is Ken Dignan, with the Christian Alternative radio program playing contemporary Christian music from now until 10:00 p.m. Stay tuned for the latest hits in contemporary gospel music."

Finally, one evening, my youngest son was playing hockey for his high school team and needed a ride to his practice. It was only a few years before the time I had to stop driving my disability equipped van.

He was in a hurry to get there, and I came down the hallway from my bedroom to the top of a ramp that linked the bedrooms over the three stairs to the main floor. It was a bit tricky to maneuver my power scooter to turn and go down the ramp.

In too much of a hurry, I didn't realize my speed would make me unable to make the turn properly and catapulted the scooter right off the ramp like Evil Knievel. My scooter went flying, and I flew off it, bouncing my head off the laminate kitchen floor.

I was knocked out a few seconds and lay on the floor. My son ran next door to get help from the neighbor man, who hurried over to assist my son in getting me up and seated on a kitchen chair. My neighbor called an ambulance.

Though I'd received a multitude of concussions, this was one of the worst. I was unable to remember what I had been doing and where I had been going. What time was it? What had I had for dinner? Everything was hazy.

By the time the ambulance got there, I was thinking more clearly. I remembered what was going on. Because of the temporary memory loss and the caution of a possible concussion, I was taken to the hospital by ambulance.

I remember imagining, *Now what are the neighbors thinking?* The thoughts about the neighbors continued. *Is that ambulance for that handicapped guy? Is he all right? I was wondering how long he'd make it.*

Fall after fall drove me to Christ, and I gave Him my hurts, pains, and suffering. I had to depend on Him to protect me and send people to assist me with my daily vital and essential needs. As I look back, I clearly see that God has always helped me get through. His invisible, unseen hand has used many people to pick me up and keep on going forward, allowing me to be productive and live for His glory.

Coming Close to Getting Discharged for Home

The same God who had been with me through all my falls was going to be the same God with me as it was finally coming closer for me to get discharged from the rehab center/nursing home. Even though I was praying to be able to go to my own home, a few members of my family wanted to check out and see if an assisted living center would keep the costs more economical than paying caregivers at home.

But deep down I was hoping to get back home. In any event my faith was getting stronger as I saw the potential of things happening to get me the care I needed. I knew God was not done with me yet. I was definitely living on borrowed time for a reason. I knew the Lord had a plan and purpose to continue using me, so I kept praying I'd be able to live back at home soon.

Fortunately, after looking closely at all the options from assisted living and nursing home facilities, my wife and sons began to discuss ways they could hire enough caregivers to make it possible for me to come home.

My wife and sons were able to contact a few caregivers and met them. After they met it looked like we were on the road to getting me closer to home. These caregivers became the first building blocks to assist my initial needs for the care I'd require. Money was not going to be easy to come by, however we decided to step out in faith and believe that God would provide for our needs.

Slowly but surely it appeared things were coming together to make it possible for me to live at our home. I realize not everyone in my condition or predicament may have the ability or resources to be able to stay out of a nursing home, rehab center, or assisted living facility. These can provide much needed care and resources for people who have nowhere else to turn or have unique needs that cannot be met at home.

I've had to rely on my family whom the Lord has used throughout my whole life. I'd have to continue depending on assistance from my wife and sons. Two are married, and their spouses are a great support. My five brothers, two sisters, and their families all remain supportive, along with my wife's, and do whatever they can to assist me as well.

Despite my suffering many physical ailments and chronic pain throughout my life, God has definitely blessed me with more than money can buy through family and friends. My prayer was that there would be an adequate amount of money for caregivers, and a support group to be there physically, so I could successfully live at home. I thought, *I hope I will be "arriving home" soon.*

CHAPTER 10

Arriving Home

Rarely do adjustments in life come easily. The journey, this side of Heaven, resembles a wild ride on a roller coaster. People who have more struggles and suffering usually have to make more adjustments.

That being the case, I try not to get too high or too low, too excited or too down, because if you do, in my case, you'll keep falling flat on your face. I was seeing realistic signs, circumstances, and situations that things were coming into place to make it a reality that I'd be able to live at home soon.

The Day to Come Home Finally Arrived

I had been humbled and uplifted by the many well wishes and prayers that had gone up on my behalf during this health scare. God truly had mercy on me and spared my life for His glory. He stabilized my vitals and gave me strength to be able to serve Him longer in this world. We are encouraged to follow the prayer Jesus taught His disciples and what He prayed before His crucifixion: "Your Kingdom come, your will be done, on earth as it is in Heaven" (Matthew 6:10, 26:42). God's will allowed me to come home.

The day finally arrived for me to go home. My son Patrick and his wife, Jennifer, were able to pick me up. It was a brisk, sunshiny day. Needless to say, there were challenges.

Because of the aides' busy schedules, they could not arrange to help me get ready for my departure. When my son and his wife got to my room, you guessed it: I was not dressed and ready to leave.

I told Patrick where everything was so he could assist me. He began, and then finally one of the aides was able to show up. I got ready to go and was helped into my power wheelchair. On my way out, I said my goodbyes to all the nurses, aides, and patients I saw. Just like that I drove my motorized chair into the van, and my son and daughter-in-law drove the getaway vehicle.

A deep peace and joy fell over me. I had a sincere appreciation of what it meant to be able to go home. I felt like Dorothy in the *Wizard of Oz,* when she clicks her heels together and says, "There's no place like home. There's no place like home." I could relate to what it might feel like when a Christian passes on to their heavenly home one day to see the Lord, loved ones, and all the followers of Jesus Christ.

Sure, there were new challenges to face and difficult adjustments to make, but still, I had made it home. That was a genuine miracle and blessing from the Lord.

Being the big sports fan I am, it was cool that I made it home just in time to have a Super Bowl party two days later. It was February 5, 2012, when Super Bowl LXVI (46) took place at Lucas Oil Stadium in Indianapolis. It was between the New York Giants and the New England Patriots. The Giants won 21-17.

Thank God for the small things we can enjoy in the midst of life's trials, turmoil and testing.

As Jesus said, "So do not worry, saying, 'What shall we eat?' or 'What shall we drink?' or 'What shall we wear?' For the pagans run after all these things, and your heavenly Father knows that you need them. But seek first his kingdom and his righteousness, and all these things will be given to you as well. Therefore do not worry about tomorrow, for tomorrow will worry about itself. Each day has enough trouble of its own" (Matthew 6:31-34).

I spent that first weekend home visiting a lot with my wife, my family, and my friends. Of course I had the time of my life seeing and spending time with my two granddaughters, ages three and seven months, whom I had seen only once in those thirty-five days.

What a genuine blessing it was that God not only kept me alive, but helped me get through all the time of recuperation and now allowed me to live back in my own home.

Establishing the Care Team

We had enough caregivers, family members, and friends who assisted me in getting acclimated and established at home. I would be able to go out whenever I wanted. I could be involved with various ministries and attend worship services. Though I still faced suffering because of my disability and other ailments, being at home put me in a much better situation to deal with it.

Eventually, we were able to see what types of caregivers were needed. We were able to get established and well situated to add the right ones to my care team.

After a month or two of being home, we had a wonderful group of caregivers helping me and my family. I was extremely thankful to be home and able to stabilize my health.

I wouldn't have gotten to this place without the love, care and support of my wife, Joni. Being a disabled marriage partner creates many unique challenges and inconveniences. All marriages face difficulties along with blessings and joys. Adding a disability to a marriage brings a whole new set of circumstances.

What a loving and tireless wife Joni has been. She has been the greatest support and one of the brightest spots in my life. "For better or worse, in sickness and in health" is a part of our wedding vows that has become a cornerstone of our life together. She is a tremendous example to our sons of what it means to be a godly wife and mother. I greatly admire her and believe she is as true a follower of Jesus Christ as anyone I've ever met.

I couldn't have asked for a better life companion. We've been able to make adjustments and show tremendous flexibility and patience. I attribute all of this to the fact that both of us brought our commitment to our Lord and Savior Jesus Christ and His word into our marriage at the outset. It is by the very power and grace of God we've been able to survive the suffering and many ups and downs we have had to face. I know He'll continue to be with us until we're called home to be with Him in Heaven.

I was able to devote quality time reaching out to individuals with prayer, scripture devotionals and insights. I was communicating via my ministry website, various social media avenues, visiting area churches and writing.

God Will Comfort You So You Can Comfort Others

Are you ever ready for detours in the road? I don't think so. Yet whatever happens, it helps to keep spiritually focused with a biblical mind-set. It's amazing for me to look back and see all that God has brought me through so far. God has encouraged me, strengthened me, and led me every step of the way as I applied Scripture after Scripture, truth upon truth, and verse upon verse from the Bible.

There is a portion of Scripture in 2 Corinthians that applies here:

> Praise be to the God and Father of our Lord Jesus Christ, the Father of compassion and the God of all comfort, who comforts us in all our troubles, so that we can comfort those in any trouble with the comfort we ourselves receive from God. For just as we share abundantly in the sufferings of Christ, so also our comfort abounds through Christ. If we are distressed, it is for your comfort and salvation; if we are comforted, it is for your comfort, which produces in you patient endurance of the same sufferings we suffer. And our hope for you is firm, because we know that just

as you share in our sufferings, so also you share in our comfort.

We do not want you to be uninformed, brothers and sisters, about the troubles we experienced in the province of Asia. We were under great pressure, far beyond our ability to endure, so that we despaired of life itself. Indeed, we felt we had received the sentence of death. But this happened that we might not rely on ourselves but on God, who raises the dead. He has delivered us from such a deadly peril, and he will deliver us again. On him we have set our hope that he will continue to deliver us, as you help us by your prayers. Then many will give thanks on our behalf for the gracious favor granted us in answer to the prayers of many. (2 Corinthians 1:3-11)

This passage tells us that God allows our suffering to show forth His comforting and sustaining power in us. We can encourage someone else to receive that same comfort by seeing how we made it through with God's power and grace. I can trust that my story of how God helped me will give others faith and hope that He'll help them in the same manner.

This passage reveals that God brings challenges into our lives to remind us not to rely on ourselves but upon Him. The key is not to lose hope and to continually believe that the Lord will deliver you time and time again. You in turn will be able to offer encouragement, advice, wisdom, prayer, and comfort to others, which will assist them in coping successfully with their suffering.

Suffering Can Cause a Healthy Dependence

Whether it was my father, mother, brothers, sisters, the extended family, or my wife and children, God has never let me be alone. He's graciously used friends, acquaintances, and even strangers to help me throughout college, seminary, and the various churches I've served as pastor. When I couldn't do for myself, the Lord graciously provided others to come alongside of me each step of the way.

I was raised to believe in God and develop a relationship with Jesus Christ. All of my experiences have taught me to trust in God no matter what. This helped me foster a genuine faith throughout my life.

The Bible tells us that "without faith it is impossible to please God. For they that come to Him must believe that He exists and rewards those who diligently seek Him" (Hebrews 11:6). It also says "The righteous will live by faith" (Galatians 3:11).

We must depend on the Lord to give us the faith we need and to help it grow as we obey and stay close to Him. The Word says, "It is by grace you have been saved by faith and this faith is a gift from God. You didn't earn it as it is a gift from God so you can't boast about it" (Ephesians 2:8).

Jesus constantly told us not to worry or fear about things that were out of our control. Look at what He said in the Gospels: "Who of you by worrying can add a single hour to his life? Since you cannot do this very little thing, why do you worry about the rest?" (Luke 12:25-26).

Peter, who knew about emotional and physical suffering, said, under the inspiration of the Holy Spirit, "Cast all your anxiety on Him because He cares for you" (1 Peter 5:7).

Solomon, who had all the wisdom and blessings God could offer, lost it all by his pride and disobedience. Yet he was able to describe a life right with the Lord when he said, "When you lie down, you will not be afraid; when you lie down, your sleep will be sweet" (Proverbs 3:24).

Jesus knows this world had many ups and downs. He understands life is not fair but that all will equal out in heaven where, symbolically, believers will stand on level ground at the foot of His cross.

Suffering can have a silver lining by causing you not to be so selfish and preoccupied with yourself. Carrying the weight of the world on your own shoulders, all by yourself, usually leads to anxiety, worry, and frustration. But suffering has a way of keeping you humbly dependent on God and others.

By depending heavily on God, you can receive a special blessing of divine peace and comfort. It comes from knowing you're not by yourself. You have someone guiding you each step of the way. I sure did as God, my family and friends all helped me get home from the hospital and rehab center.

Suffering Comes to Strip You of Selfishness

The New Testament teaches that your body is not your own. Your life and time is not your own. 1 Corinthians 6:19-20 says, "Do you not know that your bodies are temples of the Holy Spirit, who is in you, whom you have received from God? You are not your own; you were bought at a price. Therefore honor God with your bodies." Difficult life situations can and will come to everyone.

Suffering comes to remind us to be on guard against pride. God designed suffering to teach us that what happens in this life is ultimately preparing us to live for Heaven and the world to come.

James Emery White, whom I quoted earlier, tells us that the desert in the Bible is often a symbol for times of suffering:

> You've probably been in a desert or two yourself, times when there was little to bolster your self-esteem. The desert is a season when you feel emptied of any and all sense of worth, accomplishment or merit. Your ego is parched. It's a strong word, but the desert is the place of breaking, when you are broken down in ways that are excruciatingly humbling and often painful. But from the brokenness you are able to hear God with the utmost clarity, because pride and pretense have been silenced. (1)

Jesus Took My Place on the Cross

A theme that resonates in this book is that God allows suffering to keep you humble and trusting in Him more than in yourself. Suffering is God's greatest tool to mold you into His image. No one likes to hear this or believe it. Yet as you've been seeing, Scripture teaches it cover to cover.

In my case, I know God spared my life to keep me on earth for a reason. I recognize I'm living on borrowed time, extra time He has allotted to me. He could have taken me home on December 31, 2011, or January 1, 2012. True to His nature, He can have a plan for me that is different from his plan for someone else. He wanted to remind me that Christ took my place when He died on the cross. He took God's wrath I deserved for my sin. I would not have to die a spiritual death but have eternal life. "But God demonstrates His own love for us in this: While we were still sinners, Christ died for us" (Romans 5:8).

Galatians 2:20 says, "I have been crucified with Christ and I no longer live, but Christ lives in me. The life I now live in the body, I live by faith in the Son of God, who loved me and gave himself for me." When Jesus took our place and sacrificed His life on the cross for us, it meant that those who turn their lives over to Him die to self and live to a new eternal life.

That's what baptism teaches a believer as it says in Romans 6:3-4: "Don't you know that all of us who were baptized into Christ Jesus were baptized into his death? We were therefore buried with him through baptism into death in order that, just as Christ was raised from the dead through the glory of the Father, we too may live a new life."

"The righteous cry out, and the LORD hears, and delivers them out of all their troubles" (Psalm 34:17 [NKJV]). The Bible shows us that God does not promise to keep you from experiencing any problems or troubles. In fact, Jesus told us, "In this life we will experience many trials and tribulations, but we should be of good cheer because He has overcome the world" (John 16:33).

We Can Be More Than Conquerors in Our Suffering

A dynamic portion of Scripture comes to mind that clearly addresses this truth. It's found in Romans 8:31-39:

> If God is for us, who can be against us? He who did not spare his own Son, but gave him up for us all—how will he not also, along with him, graciously give us all things? Who will bring any charge against those whom God has chosen? It is God who justifies. Who then is the one who condemns? No one. Christ Jesus who died—more than that, who was raised to life—is at the right hand of God and is also interceding for us. Who shall separate us from the love of Christ? Shall trouble or hardship or persecution or famine or nakedness or danger or sword? As it is written; For your sake we face death all day long; we are considered as sheep to be slaughtered.
>
> No, in all these things we are more than conquerors through him who loved us.

> For I am convinced that neither death
> nor life, neither angels nor demons,
> neither the present nor the future, nor
> any powers, neither height nor depth, nor
> anything else in all creation, will be able
> to separate us from the love of God that
> is in Christ Jesus our Lord.

Many followers of Christ have been able to endure physical suffering from illness, torture, accidents, or emotional suffering caused by persecution, imprisonment, or martyrdom. Nothing has been able to separate them from the love of God that is in Christ Jesus our Lord.

The truths of this passage are echoed by Christian believers throughout church history. Some ministers wrote about their lives and theology while others were written about during the ages. Those who died for their faith were called martyrs. Regardless, all the others were faithful and dedicated followers of Christ. They lived sacrificial lives on earth but were blessed beyond measure as they entered the glories of Heaven. Even though some were young and in their prime at death, meant nothing, as soon as they saw Jesus.

These are people like Justin Martyr, Augustine, Thomas Aquinas, Francis of Assisi, John Owen, David Brainerd, and the list goes on. Here are a few of them:

John Owen (1616-1683) was an English theologian and "was without doubt not only the greatest theologian of the English Puritan movement but also one of the greatest European Reformed theologians of his day, and quite possibly possessed the finest theological mind that England ever produced." (2)

He was a prolific writer who wrote many theological articles about how God allows suffering and uses it in this life to cause us to surrender our heart and will to Christ's glory. He lived his life longing to go to heaven and be with his Lord Jesus. The Rev. Owen got through life living for heaven and not this world. He wrote a great message called *The Glory of Christ*.

Here is a quote from it: "On Christ's glory I would fix all my thoughts and desires, and the more I see of the glory of Christ, the more the painted beauties of this world will wither in my eyes and I will be more and more crucified to this world. It will become to me like something dead and putrid, impossible for me to enjoy" (3).

David Brainerd, a missionary to the Indians in Massachusetts in 1727, died at age twenty-seven of tuberculosis. He tirelessly dedicated his life to serving God in the midst of suffering and sacrifice for the "glory of God" (4).

Jonathan Edwards, his father-in-law, wrote his biography in 1749, and it's been in print since then. It has affected and changed many lives to serve God wholeheartedly no matter what, notably, well-known missionaries and ministers such as David Livingston, William Carey, Jim Elliot, Andrew Murray, and countless others (5).

Robert Murray McCheyne from Scotland experienced the heartache of two broken engagements. He too was familiar with pain and suffering and embraced it for God's glory. McCheyne found God's comfort to be enough to keep him serving the Lord faithfully. He also died at an early age: twenty-nine. Here is one of his often quoted prayers: "Lord, make me as holy as a pardoned sinner can be made." This prayer shows us the ultimate surrender he had to the Lord (6).

Besides the aforementioned, this book couldn't hold the names of all the godly and righteous Christians throughout the ages who have suffered greatly according to the will of God. Many experienced tremendous hardships and sacrifices, gracefully accepting the road of suffering for the glory of God.

I have to mention the names of two talented and blessed musicians who sang and wrote prolific worship and Scripture songs from the 1970s, '80s, and '90s. They died untimely deaths and were killed in accidents at an early age. Keith Green, twenty-nine (October 21, 1953-July 28, 1982) and Rich

Mullins, forty-two (October 21, 1955-September 19, 1997) were American gospel singers, songwriters, musicians, and contemporary Christian music artists. Look up their songs and read about their lives, and you'll see the impact they made and left behind in the will of God (7).

Untimely deaths from illnesses, accidents, and tragedies are all part of life in this fallen world. It shouldn't surprise us, because this world is under the curse of sin. However the most important question everyone must consider is, where will you spend eternity after you die? Heaven is promised to everyone who believes and trusts in Jesus Christ.

> Jesus said, "Do not let your hearts be troubled. You believe in God; believe also in me. My Father's house has many rooms; if that were not so, would I have told you that I am going there to prepare a place for you? And if I go and prepare a place for you, I will come back and take you to be with me that you also may be where I am. You know the way to the place where I am going."

> Thomas said to him, "Lord, we don't know where you are going, so how can we know the way?" Jesus answered, "I am the way and the truth and the life. No

one comes to the Father except through me." (John 14:1-6)

Ever since I came to know Jesus, "the way, the truth and the life," I've had a genuine peace in my soul. I came to believe everything the Bible taught about heaven and it was vividly implanted into my mind. It prepared my heart to accept whatever God planned for my life day by day.

Suffering Will Touch Everyone at Some Time

It is clearly taught in Scripture that trouble will come to everyone. This is a fact of life touched on by Jesus in the Sermon on the Mount. Matthew 5:45 says, "The rain will fall on the just and unrighteous alike." Storm clouds hit everyone. The difference for a believer in Christ is the foundation on which your life is built. Matthew 7:24-27 tells us to build our lives on the foundation of God's word so when the storms of life come, the house will not fall down, because of its firm foundation.

So remember that bad things can happen to good Christian people, and good things can happen to non-believers and even evil and harmful people or visa-versa. The Bible tells us that circumstances may occur to make it seem as though God is not fair. But ultimately God has promised His children when they get to heaven they'll, "understand it better by and by," as the old hymn states.

We see this truth principle clearly in the following Bible passage:

> The time came when the beggar (Lazarus) died and the angels carried him to Abraham's side. The rich man also died and was buried. In Hades, where he was in torment, he looked up and saw Abraham far away, with Lazarus by his side. So he called to him, "Father Abraham, have pity on me and send Lazarus to dip the tip of his finger in water and cool my tongue, because I am in agony in this fire." But Abraham replied, "Son, remember that in your lifetime you received your good things, while Lazarus received bad things, but now he is comforted here and you are in agony." (Luke 16:22-25)

Heaven will be the only place where the "fairness ground" will be balanced out. In Heaven you will never hear anyone say, "It's not fair." Everyone will finally be fulfilled and in a great place where they will understand everything. There will be no jealousy, selfishness, pride, or ego.

All of our suffering will become a distant memory in the light of an eternity in the kingdom of God, in our glorified bodies that will last forever—bodies that will never grow old, get sick, or know suffering. We will be thankful for anything God used to prepare us for His kingdom.

The great hope is finding fulfillment, joy, and peace from the Lord and Savior, Jesus Christ. Submitting your life to God will give you the greatest, most remarkable rewards. The majority of these rewards will come to believers in Heaven when God honors His children with crowns and blessings.

While we're on earth, every so often we should pray for God to periodically give us "a glimpse of Heaven." Keeping your eyes on the reward and blessing of heaven should comfort and sustain every child of God when they face trials and suffering.

CHAPTER 11

A Glimpse of Heaven

Much has been written about "near death" experiences. I've read some of these accounts and a few look very interesting and intriguing.

Yet I know they can also lead to skepticism. Secular and liberal-minded individuals say Heaven and life after death are improbable if not impossible. They say it is "fairy tale-like." To them, it sounds nice and too good to be true, and it's wishful thinking.

However, I take the Bible to be a literal, accurate, and inspired book. The Scriptures speak volumes about heaven and the afterlife. That's why Christian believers have been able to face all kinds of suffering, because they knew this world was just the waiting room for heaven.

Death and going to Heaven took on an even deeper meaning to me when I lost my twenty-year-old son to an early departure from this world. I looked forward to being reunited with him.

Suffering the Loss of Our Son

My wife and I had to deal with the suffering of an untimely death of a child. It was during a time when our third son, Ryan, was going through some very trying circumstances. He developed into a bright student and talented, hardworking athlete.

While attending high school, he received great grades for his classes. As a freshman, he played football and baseball for his large high school of 4,000 students. In his sophomore year, he competed in football and wrestling.

He excelled in everything he did. By his junior year, he qualified for Advanced Placement courses that were college level. Ryan rarely got any score lower than an A or B, mostly A's. Athletically he continued to do well. He was highly driven to attain good grades and excel in athletics with the hope of a possible scholarship from a college.

Then halfway through his junior year, he began acting very moody. He would lose his temper and have a difficult time controlling himself. There were times when he would become extremely paranoid and think other students or friends were talking about or avoiding him. That contributed to hindering his normal ability to get along with others, which occasionally caused him to get into fights.

He began threatening suicide. He often said he didn't want to live anymore and wished he would die. After a few suicide attempts and other serious behavioral problems, along with dropping out of school, we had him hospitalized. Tests revealed he was suffering from bipolar disorder.

One of the toughest kinds of suffering is seeing your child hurting so badly. He didn't want to live. There were many ups and downs during the next four years. It was struggle after struggle, hurt after hurt, three steps forward and two steps back.

Sadly on December 14, 2002, our dear son Ryan died from suicide by hanging himself in our basement. My wife discovered his body around 5:00 a.m.

I chronicle our painful details in my book *Ryan's Story*. There's no greater and longer-lasting pain than losing a child to death, and suicide intensifies the grief.

Because of the stigma about suicide I knew some Christians and churches had questions like: *Doesn't God consider death by suicide a murder, thus breaking the sixth commandment "Thou shalt not kill?" How can someone who kills himself by suicide go to Heaven?*

These questions reveal a true lack of understanding about the topic of suicide. Biblically, psychologically and medically, suicide is a delicate and in-depth subject. The majority of individuals who die from suicide have some type of chemical imbalance that causes a physical and emotional disorder whether it was diagnosed or not.

There is a lot of helpful research available to assist with the awareness and prevention of suicide. You can check out organizations like the *American Foundation of Suicide Prevention* and the *American Association of Suicidology.*

I miss my son daily. Even though it's been many years since he has passed on to Heaven, a day does not go by when I don't think of him or feel a twinge down in my heart because he's left this earth.

I wonder, What would he be like today? Whom would he have married? He loved kids and animals, so how many kids and dogs would he have?

I say it's an ache that never goes away. All you can do is cope with the pain by receiving God's comfort and the promises of Scripture. "Even though I walk through the darkest valley, I will fear no evil, for you are with me; your rod and your staff, they comfort me" (Psalm 23:4).

The reality of it all was that it happened and somehow with God's grace we had to go on for our family and the memory of our son. Heaven became a much more inviting place, of course, realizing I'd be with Jesus, but also knowing I'd see my son Ryan again.

Yes, I believe my son is in Heaven because he believed in Christ and trusted Him as his Lord and Savior. He became ill and developed a chemical imbalance which led to the diagnosis of bipolar disorder. This type of medical condition produces deep, dark, relentless depression, which long-term, can cause a person to lose all hope. At this stage it's not that one really wants to kill himself, which would devastate their loved ones. Instead they are desperate to kill and stop their pain, thus some resort to death by suicide. Ultimately we must commit the final answers to this sensitive issue to God's mercy and grace, entrusting our loved ones into His hands.

False Doctrine Can Make Suffering Even More Difficult

I must spend a small portion addressing the dangers of wrong thinking that can lead to believing false doctrine. There are some Bible scholars and preachers who teach that with the right kind of faith and Bible knowledge, you are able to receive every miracle of healing or prosperity requested. These teach that any prayer offered in true faith is guaranteed a positive result. One can receive the ability to sidestep suffering, gain wealth and live to a ripe old age of seventy or better.

Sadly, I believe they are very misled and inaccurately interpret the Bible.

Admittedly, I believe the Scriptures reveal a God who can and will perform miracles of healing, provisions, protection, and prosperity, as stated in previous chapters. There are numerous instances of divine intervention in the Bible. Great servants of the Lord felt comfortable crying out to God in prayer when they needed any type of miracle and divine intervention.

Whether they received whatever they asked for or not didn't really matter. They were convinced that God had the authority and right to exercise and impose His will in every situation. If a miracle took place, God was praised. If a miracle did not take place as so requested, God was still praised.

The book of Hebrews has a passage that illustrates this:

> I do not have time to tell about Gideon, Barak, Samson and Jephthah, about David and Samuel and the prophets, who through faith conquered kingdoms, administered justice, and gained what was promised; who shut the mouths of lions, quenched the fury of the flames, and escaped the edge of the sword; whose weakness was turned to strength;

and who became powerful in battle and routed foreign armies. Women received back their dead, raised to life again.

There were others who were tortured, refusing to be released so that they might gain an even better resurrection. Some faced jeers and flogging, and even chains and imprisonment. They were put to death by stoning; they were sawed in two; they were killed by the sword. They went about in sheepskins and goatskins, destitute, persecuted and mistreated the world was not worthy of them. They wandered in deserts and mountains, living in caves and in holes in the ground.

These were all commended for their faith, yet none of them received what had been promised, since God had planned something better for us so that only together with us would they be made perfect. (Hebrews 11:32-40)

Some received tremendous miracles, others did not. Yet they were all commended for having faith in God.

Whether by Life or Death, Suffering Can Give Glory to God

I am humbled to have been kept alive by God's will thus far, especially with what I've gone through. I cannot take any credit for surviving like I have. I wouldn't have been able to make it if it hadn't been for the Lord. I can only thank God and give Him the glory that whether by life or death, I desire to show His glorious character and being.

"I consider that the sufferings of this present time are not worthy to be compared with the glory which shall be revealed in us" (Romans 8:18).

A Christian lives for God's glory and dies for God's glory. The apostle Paul speaks about this in 1 Corinthians 4:16-18: "Therefore we do not lose heart. Though outwardly we are wasting away, yet inwardly we are being renewed day by day; for our light and momentary troubles are achieving for us an eternal glory that far outweighs them all. So we fix our eyes not on what is seen, but on what is unseen, since what is seen is temporary, but what is unseen is eternal."

Hebrews 12:1-2 says, "Therefore we also, since we are surrounded by so great a cloud of witnesses, let us lay aside every weight, and the sin which so easily ensnares us, and let us run with endurance the race that is set before us, looking unto Jesus, the author and finisher of our faith, who for the joy that was set before Him endured the cross, despising the shame, and has sat down at the right hand of the throne of God."

Genuine believers are called to lay aside any hindrances to their walk in Christ. They are told to run the Christian life with endurance like they're in a race. There will be many challenges, because this race is like a long-distance marathon, not a sprint. It is best to keep looking ahead, not looking to the right or left, but looking to the finish line. In this case that is Jesus, and looking away may distract you.

We can be motivated to handle whatever God sends our way by looking to that crowd of witnesses who have gone on before us. It's much like in the sporting arena, where athletes are inspired to compete and play harder when they're playing at their home field or court. The fans, cheering them on, cause them to play at a higher level.

Regardless of how difficult or challenging one's life might be, the truth is that every believer can be spurred on to "fight the fight of faith," knowing that Heaven is the finish line.

Earth Has Sorrow, Heaven Has Blessings

Notice that the only place you will really find peace and a safe place is in surrendering your heart, mind, thoughts, and desires to Jesus Christ. In Jesus you will have peace. This peace means harmony, wholeness, and a secure feeling that everything will be all right. Many things in this world will try to rob you of peace, such as anxiety, depression, discouragement, jealousy, anger, bitterness and other negative characteristics and emotions.

We must always remember this life wasn't meant to be your main stop. It's not your final destination. In fact, you are supposed to just be passing through. Jesus told you not to set up all your treasures in this life, but to store up treasures in Heaven. That's where your genuine peace is.

Jesus has overcome sin, so you have forgiveness. Jesus overcame Satan, so in Him you are not under his curse or power. Jesus overcame death, so you don't have to die, just change your location to your Heavenly home. Jesus placed you in His church, the body of believers, so you don't have to go it alone on earth.

Christ has provided all you need to live with peace in this trouble-filled world. We are put on earth to prepare us for Heaven. So to have more peace on earth, live more for Heaven.

Jesus and Life After Death

What did Jesus say about life after death? Is this life connected to the next life? Are Heaven and the afterlife just wishful thinking, or is there evidence that it exists?

The Old Testament Jewish writings and the New Testament Church writings that make up the Holy Bible, all speak of and promise immortality and life after death.

"What will it profit a man to gain the whole world and lose his own soul?" (Mark 8:36).

There is something innate in every human being that something follows after the grave. There is an awe and speculation that this life is not all there is.

Most of us feel life has to have some type of meaning. We have a sense we are heading somewhere. There's something deep down inside that resonates in our very being that we are more than lucky monkeys.

The theory of evolution can lead one to believe that our world is a result of random chance. Many conclude everything is temporary; whatever anyone does will end with this life. There is nothing more after you die. Your life has an on/off switch, and once it turns off, that's all there is. This does not resonate as true to anyone who listens to their heart or soul.

A deeper question should be, *Is there life before death? Is there a reason why you are alive? Is there any kind of evidence for life after death?*

Who was Jesus? Was he simply an enlightened Jewish rabbi who thought he was a messiah, or did He know and believe He was who He claimed to be? Biblical evidence shows that Christ believed He was the promised Messiah, the Anointed One and Redeemer of mankind. Look at the following verses:

Jesus told His disciples He alone had the keys to unlock the door to Heaven and eternal life. He shared a lot with them about Heaven. One of His famous sayings is found in John 3:16, which says, "For God so loved the world that he gave his one and only Son, that whoever believes in him shall not perish but have eternal life."

"I give them eternal life, and they shall never perish; no one will snatch them out of my hand" (John 10:28).

"I am the good shepherd; I know my sheep and my sheep know me; My sheep listen to my voice; I know them, and they follow me" (John 10: 14, 27).

Curiosity About the Afterlife

Surveys show people believe in an afterlife; many believe there is a God. Jesus spoke a lot about a resurrection. "A time is coming when those who have died will rise from the dead" (John 5:28). Near-death experiences give some people hope that there is an afterlife.

One does not have to study books about near death experiences, to prove there is a Heaven. There have been many books written about death and returning from death experiences for a long time. One of the most famous books about this came out in 1969 called *Death and Dying,* written by Elizabeth Kubler-Ross (1926-2004), an American Swiss psychiatrist who conducted extensive research and was a prolific writer on the subject. Though some believe many of her conclusions have natural explanations, her research broke interesting ground.

Currently, a popular one is *90 Minutes in Heaven,* by Don Piper, who was in a car accident and died. He claimed to have spent an hour and a half in Heaven and wrote this book about what he saw. It's hard to scientifically or medically verify claims like these, as they are subjective to the individuals themselves. However, one cannot prove they didn't happen either. Many of us with faith and a belief in Heaven are intrigued by stories of this nature (1).

Another one is *Heaven Is for Real,* by Todd Burpo (2), whose four-year-old son, Colton, became ill and had to have emergency surgery. He may have momentarily died during it only to be revived, or he may have had some type of vision during surgery. In any event, his father recorded many things his young child said he saw in Heaven during surgery. He spoke of facts about diseased family members that he could not have known.

Whether these accounts are true or not is hard to tell. Any arguments for or against them go back and forth like a "he said, she said" type of reasoning. There's no way to prove or genuinely disprove it. I myself feel comfortable in believing many of those who have had "life after death experiences" receive true information, otherwise unknowable, apart from being in heaven.

The Scriptures Hold the Standards for Life After Death

The only thing true Christian believers can do is hold everything about Heaven up to the light of Scripture, the Holy Bible. The Bible has stood the test of time regarding truths and teachings about Heaven, eternity, and the afterlife. Any other books outside of Scripture, about Heaven, must be held up to the standard of truth taught about life after death in the Bible.

The Bible definitely addresses these issues and speaks of a few people who had "near death" or "death" experiences who returned to life to tell about it. They are Lazarus, whom Jesus raised back to life (John 11:38-44) and the apostle Paul, who was left for dead after being stoned to death (Acts 14:19-20).

Jesus spoke a parable about the rich man and a beggar named Lazarus. Lazarus died, and Jesus said he went to heaven, giving details of consciousness and comfort (Luke 16:19-31). Jesus Christ and the apostle Peter even prayed over a dead body and the person came back to life (Matthew 9:23-26, Acts 9:40-42).

Some even had visions of being taken up to see Heaven while still alive. That was the apostle Paul (2 Corinthians 12:2-6) and the apostle John while in prison on the island of Patmos (Revelation 1 and 4).

For a clear example that reveals life after death and being able to know the identities of individuals from the past, all you have to do is read the passage referred to as "The Mount of Transfiguration." Jesus took Peter, James, and John with Him to a mountain most biblical scholars believe was Mount Tabor, as suggested by third-century scholar, Origen. Both Moses and Elijah, Old Testament prophets, appeared to Jesus. The disciples saw them and it was obviously revealed to them by Jesus who they were (Mark 9:2-8).

The New Testament has many documents with solid evidence that is hard to dispute. The Bible gives me all the proof I need to believe in and know there is an afterlife with a "Heaven to gain and a Hell to shun."

Only Jesus Rose with a Resurrection Body

Still, Jesus is our supreme example who presented evidence from his own life and resurrection that there is a realistic hope of a real Heaven and life after death.

After his crucifixion the Jewish religious leaders and Roman officials wanted to take every precaution to guard Jesus' dead body. Too much was at stake if the Apostles stole the body of Jesus and conspired to convince his followers he was raised from the dead.

The Gospels tell us that Christ was buried in a tomb, a huge, heavy stone was rolled in front of it, and soldiers stood guard day and night.

Jesus' followers went and hid; they scattered. They were devastated and living in fear. Is it possible these disciples could overrun the soldiers, remove the weighted boulder, and confront the soldiers? Obviously, the answer is no. Yet something happened at that historic tomb three days after Christ's crucifixion. Jesus arose from the dead three days afterward, in a resurrection body, never to suffer a physical death again.

Something occurred that has changed the course of history. The tomb was empty; no Jewish religious leaders could find the body of Jesus to parade down the streets of Jerusalem to disprove the claims of his disciples.

Fearful, confused, and perplexed followers seemed emboldened and energized by the claims that they had seen the risen Christ alive and risen from the dead. The Easter claims of the Christian church would echo throughout the ages that "Christ has risen."

> When the Sabbath was over, Mary Magdalene, Mary the mother of James, and Salome bought spices so that they might go to anoint Jesus' body. Very early on the first day of the week, just after sunrise, they were on their way to the tomb and they asked each other, "Who will roll the stone away from the entrance of the tomb?"
>
> But when they looked up, they saw that the stone, which was very large, had been rolled away. As they entered the tomb, they saw a young man dressed in a white robe sitting on the right side, and they were alarmed.

> "Don't be alarmed," he said. "You are
> looking for Jesus the Nazarene, who was
> crucified. He has risen! He is not here.
> See the place where they laid him. But
> go, tell his disciples." (Mark 16:1-7)

Jesus promised His followers that anyone who had faith and believed in Him would receive the promise of life after death, eternal life. "Those who receive my words will experience life after death" (John 8:52). Jesus went on to say, "I am the resurrection and the life. Whoever believes in Me, though he dies, he will live" (John 11:25).

Another point is that this earthly life is connected to the afterlife. How you live and what you do in this life does matter; it will affect your place in the afterlife.

We see this with two thieves who were crucified along with Jesus. One was unremorseful, and one recognized Jesus' innocence and his own guilt. He basically was moved to recognize something unique and special about Jesus' ability to forgive sin and grant eternal life. He could have heard Christ speak somewhere before.

This thief who was crucified with Jesus asked Him to remember him in the afterlife. Jesus told him, "Today you'll be with me in paradise" (Luke 23:40-43).

Upon Death a Believer Goes Straight to Heaven

Death is the doorway, a passage from this life to the next life. The apostle Paul reflected on his time of death in verses found in the epistle to the Philippians: "For to me, to live is Christ and to die is gain ... I desire to depart and be with Christ, which is better by far" (Philippians 1:21, 23).

1 Corinthians 5:8 tells us, "We are confident, yes, well pleased rather to be absent from the body and to be present with the Lord."

This remarkable Jewish rabbi, Saul, (Paul) fought against the truths held by Christians and gave his approval to the martyrdom of Stephen, one of the first appointed deacons of the early church. This deacon saw a revelation of Jesus prior to being stoned to death, which made him confident he'd be with the Lord immediately upon dying. (Acts 7:54-60). This rabbi, who was of the party called the Pharisees, arrested believers in Jesus and imprisoned them. He made a miraculous about-face after meeting Christ in a vision (Acts 9:3-9) and actually claimed to have been taken to see a genuine vision of heaven.

The following passage is from the apostle Paul speaking indirectly and humbly about himself:

I must go on boasting. Although there is nothing to be gained, I will go on to visions and revelations from the Lord. I know a man in Christ who fourteen years ago was caught up to the third heaven. Whether it was in the body or out of the body I do not know—God knows. And I know that this man—whether in the body or apart from the body I do not know, but God knows—was caught up to paradise and heard inexpressible things, things that no one is permitted to tell. (2 Corinthians 12:1-4)

Paul spoke of his certainty in Heaven and the afterlife. He claimed death was really like a promotion day, a graduation day, when you experience all you ever hoped for—when you receive your diploma, so to speak, your reward for all your years of hard labor.

It's much like how an author feels who finishes his manuscript after all the work, following countless hours of study and research, then to see the finished copy of his book. What a blessing and relief to get it all done and see the finished copy.

These early followers and disciples of Jesus Christ were convinced that what they believed about His resurrection and return to life after His death was true and factual. They claimed to have solid evidence that Christ visibly appeared to them after He died and they touched, hugged and listened to Him. No one could disprove it. Hundreds and eventually thousands, throughout the Church age, were willing to die for this.

Christ's Empty Tomb Is Greatest Evidence for Heaven

Let's look at what 1 John 1:1-4 tells us:

> That which was from the beginning, which we have heard, which we have seen with our eyes, which we have looked at and our hands have touched—this we proclaim concerning the Word of life. The life appeared; we have seen it and testify to it, and we proclaim to you the eternal life, which was with the Father and has appeared to us. We proclaim to you what we have seen and heard, so that you also may have fellowship with us. And our fellowship is with the Father and with his Son, Jesus Christ. We write this to make our joy complete.

The empty tomb and the claim by eyewitnesses that they actually saw Jesus in bodily form, alive after His crucifixion, death, and burial, gives ample truth that there's life after death. In fact, there were hundreds of individuals who claimed to have seen the risen Christ.

> For what I received I passed on to you as of first importance: that Christ died for our sins according to the Scriptures, that he was buried, that he was raised on the third day according to the Scriptures, and that he appeared to Cephas, and then to the Twelve. After that, he appeared to more than five hundred of the brothers and sisters at the same time, most of who are still living, though some have fallen asleep. Then he appeared to James, then to all the apostles, and last of all he appeared to me also (Paul the Apostle), as to one abnormally born. (1 Corinthians 15:3-8)

Jewish and Roman officials could not compete with so many eyewitness testimonies of Christ's resurrection. The truth of His resurrection has been meticulously and painstakingly preserved by the writers of the New Testament documents. These documents are reliable and can be trusted.(3)

Everyone dies and faces eternal judgment, according to Hebrews 9:27-28 when it says: "Just as people are destined to die once, and after that to face judgment, so Christ was sacrificed once to take away the sins of many;

and he will appear a second time, not to bear sin, but to bring salvation to those who are waiting for him."

With this being true that after death everyone faces Heaven or Hell, Paul the Apostle went on to tell the believers they can trust all the evidence about Jesus rising from the dead and put their confidence and faith in Him. "Christ has indeed been raised from the dead." (1 Corinthians 15:20) and "Death has been swallowed up in victory. Where, O death, is your victory? Where, O death, is your sting? The sting of death is sin, and the power of sin is the law. But thanks be to God! He gives us the victory through our Lord Jesus Christ." (1 Corinthians 15:54-57)

Lee Strobel, a former investigative reporter for the Chicago Sun Times wrote a book called *The Case for the Resurrection* after his wife became a Christian. It led him to investigate all the scriptural, theological and historical evidence for himself. Upon doing so he too committed his life to Jesus Christ. He said, "I reached my verdict: based on the historical data, I was convinced that Jesus not only claimed to be the Son of God, but he also validated that claim by returning from the dead." (4)

I too came to that conclusion and it changed my life, as you have been able to see. It gave me a deep peace and a profound faith in the Bible. It started me on the road to a meaningful and personal relationship with

Jesus Christ. I now have the assurance of going to Heaven when I leave this world.

Heaven Is Beyond Our Wildest Imagination

It's clear that God allowed this sinful, fallen, imperfect planet we call Earth to have beautiful mountains, waterfalls, oceans, and animals. We can be sure that heaven will have unbelievable scenery that will make the Grand Canyon, the Grand Tetons, and the Great Barrier Reef look insignificant.

The book of Psalms gives glory to God's creation with this world: "The heavens declare the glory of God; and the firmament shows His handiwork; Day unto day utters speech, and night unto night reveals knowledge. There is no speech nor language where their voice is not heard. Their line has gone out through all the earth, and their words to the end of the world" (Psalm 19:1-4 NKJV).

The book of Revelation gives us a number of glimpses of what life in heaven may look like:

> And he (an angel) carried me away in the Spirit to a mountain great and high, and showed me the Holy City, Jerusalem, coming down out of heaven from God. It shone with the glory of God, and its brilliance was like that of a very precious

jewel, like a jasper, clear as crystal. It had a great, high wall with twelve gates, and with twelve angels at the gates. On the gates were written the names of the twelve tribes of Israel. There were three gates on the east, three on the north, three on the south and three on the west. The wall of the city had twelve foundations, and on them were the names of the twelve apostles of the Lamb.

The angel who talked with me had a measuring rod of gold to measure the city, its gates and its walls. The city was laid out like a square, as long as it was wide. He measured the city with the rod and found it to be 12,000 stadia in length, and as wide and high as it is long. The angel measured the wall using human measurement, and it was 144 cubits thick. The wall was made of jasper, and the city of pure gold, as pure as glass. The foundations of the city walls were decorated with every kind of precious stone. The first foundation was jasper, the second sapphire, the third agate, the fourth emerald, the fifth onyx, the sixth ruby, the seventh chrysolite, the eighth beryl, the ninth topaz, the tenth turquoise, the eleventh jacinth, and the twelfth amethyst. The twelve gates were twelve pearls, each gate made of a single pearl. The great street of the city was of gold, as pure as transparent glass.

I did not see a temple in the city, because the Lord God Almighty and the Lamb are its temple. The city does not need the sun or the moon to shine on it, for the glory of God gives it light, and the Lamb is its lamp. The nations will walk by its light, and the kings of the earth will bring their splendor into it. On no day will its gates ever be shut, for there will be no night there. The glory and honor of the nations will be brought into it. Nothing impure will ever enter it, nor will anyone who does what is shameful or deceitful, but only those whose names are written in the Lamb's book of life. (Revelation 21:10-27)

Examine these details and see how beautiful God is making the New Heaven and Earth, along with the New Jerusalem.

You may have planets and mountains to explore. You might be able to fish and go deep-sea diving. Heaven is not going to be a boring place at all. This almighty, all-knowing, all-caring, and compassionate God desires to share everything with His redeemed creation, with those "made in His image."

This reminds me of a Scripture passage that speaks of the inheritance Christians will receive: "In Him you also trusted, after you heard the word of truth, the gospel of your salvation; in whom also, having believed, you were sealed with the Holy Spirit of promise, who is the guarantee of our inheritance until the redemption of the purchased possession, to the praise of His glory" (Ephesians 1:13-14).

Knowing There's a Heaven Helps One Handle Suffering

We, children of God, redeemed by the "blood Christ shed on the cross," can be sure we serve a God that will do "exceeding, abundantly, above and beyond all we can ever think of or even imagine." That sounds like a Scripture verse: "Now to Him who is able to do exceedingly abundantly above all that we ask or think, according to the power that works in us, to Him be glory in the church by Christ Jesus to all generations, forever and ever. Amen" (Ephesians 3:20).

Christians can receive great strength and comfort by keeping their hearts and minds on Heaven. Author Randy Alcorn, who has written a number of books about Heaven, says this:

"Set your hearts on things above, where Christ is seated at the right hand of God" (Colossians 3:1). This is a direct command to set our hearts on Heaven and to contemplate what God has promised us. And to make sure we don't miss the importance of a heaven-centered life, the next verse says, "Set your minds on things above, not on earthly things." God commands us to set our hearts and minds on Heaven.

To long for Christ, is to long for Heaven, for that is where we will be with him. God's people are "longing for a better country" (Hebrews 11:16). We cannot set our eyes on Christ without setting our eyes on Heaven, and we cannot set our eyes on Heaven without setting our eyes on Christ. Still, it is not only Christ but "things above" we are to set our minds on.

Anticipating Heaven doesn't eliminate life's pain, but it lessens it and puts it in perspective. Meditating on God's eternal promises is a great pain reliever. It reminds us that suffering and death are temporary conditions. Our existence will not end in suffering and death—they are but a gateway to our eternal life of unending joy.

The biblical doctrine of Heaven is about the future, but it has tremendous benefits here and now. If we grasp it, it will shift our center of gravity and radically change our perspective on life. This is what the Bible calls "hope," a word used six times in Romans 8:20-25, the passage in which Paul says that all creation longs for our resurrection and the world's coming redemption.

Don't place your hope in favorable circumstances, which cannot and will not last. Place your hope in Christ and his promises. He will return, and we will be resurrected to life on the New Earth, where we will behold God's face and joyfully serve him forever. (4)

The New Heaven Will End All Suffering

Heaven will be a wonderful place where there will be no more suffering, pain, crying, or hurting. I don't believe anyone in this life can get a true, graphic picture of what Heaven will be like. It will be an ever expanding, ever evolving, ever exciting kingdom, with unlimited potential and places for involvement and growth.

In the book of Revelation we see that Heaven is far more than what anyone can even imagine. Whereas this earthly life can be filled with tears, mourning, pain, and death, Heaven will be an eternal place of life, joy, and peace. There'll be no more turmoil, tragedies or accidents, no more goodbyes, no more fear, worry, or heartaches.

We will be able to share an intimate relationship with God the Father, the Son, and the Holy Spirit, along with all the saints. I use that term generally referring to all Christians whom the New Testament calls "hagios" in the Greek text for "the holy" or "the saints."

There remains so much ahead for followers of Jesus Christ. There are gifts to be given out by the Lord. There are ranks of leadership and service to be assigned by God. We shall see about "the hierarchy of Heaven and activities beyond."

CHAPTER 12

The Hierarchy of Heaven and Activities Beyond

We must understand that God uses our life as a proving ground. It serves as a spiritual boot camp. Our experiences with trials and suffering prepare us for rewards and responsibilities in the New Heaven and New Earth. Knowing this truth will better equip us to deal with pain and struggles.

A passage in Revelation teaches that God is going to create a brand New Heaven and Earth at the end of the age.

> Then I saw "a new heaven and a new earth," for the first heaven and the first earth had passed away, and there was no longer any sea. I saw the Holy City, the New Jerusalem, coming down out of heaven from God, prepared as a bride beautifully dressed for her husband. And I heard a loud voice from the throne saying, "Look! God's dwelling place is now among the people, and he will dwell with them. They will be his people, and God

himself will be with them and be their God." (Revelation 21:1-3)

These verses in Revelation intimate that God's New Heaven and New Earth will be the result of His final plan and glory. It will be the never-ending Kingdom of God.

Only God knows what it will entail. God has all the details and activities that He has desired to share with His crowned creation, "redeemed mankind made in his image." It will be a place of never-ending activities, action, and adventures.

Suffering for Christ Leads to Crowns and Conquests

The apostle Paul, whom God used to pen more than half of the New Testament documents, looked at his life like a race, like competitions in the Olympics. As the Olympics grant awards of gold, silver, and bronze, God's Word alludes to various crowns. It talks about "crowns of life," "crowns of righteousness," and more.

When Paul came to know Christ as his Messiah, Lord and Savior, he came to realize that this world was not all there is. He longed for and was looking forward to his rewards in Heaven when he said, "For I am already being poured out like a drink offering, and the time for my departure is near. I have fought the good fight, I have finished the race and I have kept the faith. Now there is in store for me the crown of righteousness, which the Lord, the righteous Judge, will award to me on that day—and not only to me, but also to all who have longed for his appearing" (2 Timothy 4:6-8).

Revelation 2:10 says, "Be faithful unto death, and I will give you the crown of life."

Dr. John Piper, who has written and preached much about suffering, said, "The crown that awaits us after death will compensate ten thousand times over for any suffering in the service of Christ" (1).

Jesus told a parable about a master and his servants. The principles here speak about rewards and responsibilities for faithful stewards:

> Again, it will be like a man going on a journey, which called his servants and entrusted his wealth to them. To one he gave five bags of gold, to another two bags, and to another one bag, each according to his ability.
>
> Then he went on his journey ... After a long time the master of those servants returned and settled accounts with them. The man who had received five bags of gold brought the other five. "Master," he

said, "you entrusted me with five bags of gold. See, I have gained five more." His master replied, "Well done, good and faithful servant! You have been faithful with a few things; I will put you in charge of many things. Come and share your master's happiness!"

The man with two bags of gold also came. "Master," he said, "you entrusted me with two bags of gold; see, I have gained two more." His master replied, "Well done, good and faithful servant! You have been faithful with a few things; I will put you in charge of many things. Come and share your master's happiness!"

Then the man who had received one bag of gold came. "Master," he said, "I knew that you are a hard man, harvesting where you have not sown and gathering where you have not scattered seed. So I was afraid and went out and hid your gold in the ground. See, here is what belongs to you." His master replied, "You wicked, lazy servant! So you knew that I harvest where I have not sown and gather where I have not scattered seed?

Well then, you should have put my money on deposit with the bankers, so that when I returned I would have received it back with interest."

So take the bag of gold from him and give it to the one who has ten bags. For whoever has will be given more and they will have abundance. Whoever does not have, even what they have will be taken from them. And throw that worthless servant outside, into the darkness, where there will be weeping and gnashing of teeth. (Matthew 25:14-15,19-30)

In this parable of Jesus, He speaks of God being like a master going on a journey who gave his servants some of his investments to invest and multiply until he came back. Two of them invested, and their investment increased.

The master said to both of them, "Well done. my good and faithful servant. I will put you in charge of many things. Enter into your master's happiness."

We see that these servants will be given various responsibilities and blessings, whereas the doubting, fearful, and lazy servant will face an eternity without the master's blessings. This is a very sobering thought.

Suffering Prepares You for Heavenly Ranking

The Bible mentions that believers will have responsibilities as they reign with Christ in Heaven. This parable says, "I will put you in charge of many things." That carries with it the idea of rank and hierarchy. The military has generals, captains, lieutenants, sergeants, and privates. Heaven may also have various positions of authority and accountability. However, the rankings will not denote power and authority over others in Heaven, because God has all the power and authority. It will deal with responsibilities and duties for God's kingdom.

Not that everyone who has believed in Christ and received His forgiving grace should worry or be upset that they may be ordered around by fellow followers of Christ during eternity. That's not what I mean to communicate here.

God has the ability and power to set up an eternal kingdom where everyone will get along. No one who bows to the King of Kings and Lord of Lords will lord their position over anybody. They may function in different places of authority or responsibility, serving in whatever capacity God places them. Heaven will definitely be a kingdom where everyone is going to live in harmony and love God along with all the saints.

I understand this can be a difficult concept for many of us to understand or conceive of with the mind-set we have on earth and the way we currently live. It diminishes the awesomeness of Heaven to visualize it as a dull place with nothing to do except sing hymns and lay on clouds listening to God preach sermons.

Broaden your horizons and imagination, read between the lines and think outside the box. Even in the angelic realm there seems to be a hierarchy of various positions (1 Peter 3:22). Angels are referred to as archangels, seraphim, and cherubim (Psalm 99:1, Isaiah 6:2,9, Jude 1:9). Some angels act as guardian angels for God's children and protect them and even look after small children (Matthew 18:10).

Satan's realm of evil spirits has a hierarchy, as we see in Ephesians 6:12, which says, "For our struggle is not against flesh and blood, but against the rulers, against the authorities, against the powers of this dark world and against the spiritual forces of evil in the heavenly realms." Rulers, authorities, powers, and spiritual forces in heavenly realms speak of various hierarchies.

Christ Will Judge a Believer's Conduct

Jesus will act as a type of Olympic judge. He will distribute and delegate the various crowns and places of authority to help Him rule and reign in God's kingdom. During Paul's day the Olympic-type judges sat on the "bema seat" so they could clearly see all the competitors compete and get a visual of the different places they finished. (2)

> Do you not know that in a race all the runners run, but only one gets the prize? Run in such a way as to get the prize. Everyone who competes in the games goes into strict training. They do it to get a crown that will not last, but we do it to get a crown that will last forever. Therefore I do not run like someone running aimlessly; I do not fight like a boxer beating the air. No, I strike a blow to my body and make it my slave so that after I have preached to others, I myself will not be disqualified for the prize. (1 Corinthians 9:24-27)

> By the grace God has given me, I laid a foundation as a wise builder, and someone else is building on it. But each one should build with care. For no one can lay any foundation other than the one already laid, which is Jesus Christ. If anyone builds on this foundation using gold, silver, costly stones, wood, hay or straw, their work will be shown for what it is, because the Day will bring it to light. It will be revealed with fire, and the fire will test the quality of each person's work. If what has been

> built survives, the builder will receive a reward. If it is burned up, the builder will suffer loss but yet will be saved—even though only as one escaping through the flames. (1 Corinthians 3:10-15)

This passage contains symbolism of the judgment seat where Christ will test the way a believer lived their life for Him. It will not be a judgment like the "great white throne," a judgment in the end of time of whether someone's name was written in the Book of Life, giving him permission to enter Heaven. This is not a judgment for eternal life but for rewards and crowns.

You see rewards mentioned here in Matthew when Jesus refers to the end of the age: "For the Son of Man is going to come in his Father's glory with his angels, and then he will reward each person according to what they have done" (Matthew 25:31).

Therefore this could be the time and place where Jesus Christ thanks and congratulates His followers for facing great trials, sufferings, and possible martyrdom. The believers will cheer on these saints, applauding them in heartfelt appreciation and joy for their godly sacrifice and example to endure terrible times of suffering humbly and graciously for the glory of God.

"If we suffer, we shall also reign with him" (2 Timothy 2:12).

You have made them to be a kingdom and priests to serve our God, and they will reign" (Romans 5:17).

These concepts and Scriptures clearly illustrate that God uses our sufferings to prepare us for crowns, rewards, and responsibilities that come to fruition in heaven. It bears repeating again: I'm convinced heaven is not just a place where Christians will sit on clouds with angels and halos, strumming on harps, singing songs to God, and listening to Jesus share long sermons and teachings for an eternity. God deserves the benefit of the doubt on that.

Now don't get me wrong, there's nothing wrong with singing praises to and worshipping the Lord and Savior Jesus Christ. We will have an eternity to participate in choirs of adoration to the Alpha and Omega, which means the God of the beginning and the end. Heaven will be far more creative and glorious, with unfathomable exploits, expeditions, and encounters of the eternal kind.

Why can't God's New Heaven and Earth be such a place where there will be new assignments, new things to learn, new responsibilities for leadership, new adventures, and places to be explored? Who knows, but the Almighty alone, what is planned for His holy bride, the church? These words of symbolic depth carry with it wonder, fulfillment, and unending joy.

Rejoicing for Honors and Rewards

In this letter to the churches in Ephesus and the surrounding area, Paul spoke about the symbolism of the Church as the bride of Christ:

> Husbands, love your wives, just as Christ loved the church and gave himself up for her to make her holy, cleansing her by the washing with water through the word, and to present her to himself as a radiant church, without stain or wrinkle or any other blemish, but holy and blameless. In this same way, husbands ought to love their wives as their own bodies. He who loves his wife loves himself. After all, no one ever hated their own body, but they feed and care for their body, just as Christ does the church—for we are members of his body. For this reason a man will leave his father and mother and be united to his wife, and the two will become one flesh. This is a profound mystery—but I am talking about Christ and the church. (Ephesians 5:25-32)

"Let us rejoice and be glad and give him glory! For the wedding of the Lamb has come, and his bride has made herself ready" (Revelation 19:7).

As the bride of Christ, believers will be adorned to serve Him actively and participate in duties with Him in the kingdom of God.

There will be no envy or harmful attitudes in heaven. If one person went through more suffering than another on earth and receives more crowns and rewards than another who didn't suffer as much, everyone will totally understand and be good with it, because there will be no bitterness, jealousy, or anger.

Everyone in Heaven will rejoice and be thankful to see God give various honors and certain responsibilities of authority to those who suffered more in life and did so for the glory and honor of His kingdom. Heaven will be a place of one big happy family, something that we who are still on earth can hardly conceive of with our finite minds.

The redeemed of Heaven will have new ways of thinking, a new mind-set, a new frame of reference altogether. When the genuine followers of God get to Heaven, His plan and purposes, which have been written in eternity, are going to come to pass. There will be no more sin and selfishness. Heaven's population will truly be able to "rejoice with those who rejoice" (1 Corinthians 12:29).

Godly Suffering: Earth's Boot Camp for Heaven

Author Max Lucado says this about suffering:

> Certain chapters in this life seem so unnecessary—like nostrils on the pre-born. Like suffering. Loneliness. Disease. Holocausts. Martyrdom. Hurricanes, earthquakes and monsoons.
>
> If we assume this world exists just for pre-grave happiness, these atrocities disqualify it from doing so! But what if this earth is the womb? Might these challenges, severe as they may be, serve to prepare us, equip us for the world to come?
>
> The apostle Paul wrote in 2nd Corinthians 4:17: "*'These little troubles are getting us ready for an eternal glory that will make all our troubles seem like nothing."*
>
> 'Eternal glory?' I'd like a large cup of that, wouldn't you?
>
> Everything in this life is preparing us for the next. (3)

Author, scholar, and minister Eugene Peterson translates this passage in his version of the New Testament called *The Message* this way:

> So we're not giving up. How could we! Even though on the outside it often looks like things are falling apart on us, on the inside, where God is making new life, not a day goes by without his unfolding grace. These hard times are small potatoes compared to the coming good times, the lavish celebration prepared for us. There's far more here than meets the eye. The things we see now are here today, gone tomorrow. But the things we can't see now will last forever. (2 Corinthians 4:16-18)

We may not like this answer to why God allows suffering, but it makes sense when you think about it. This life serves as a training ground that prepares us for an eternity in Heaven. The world of suffering and pain; disappointments and heartaches; catastrophes and accidents; all come to develop our faith, character, humility, and trust in God.

The Bible says, "Endure suffering along with me, as a good soldier of Christ Jesus. Soldiers don't get tied up in the affairs of civilian life, for then they cannot please the officer who enlisted them. And athletes cannot win the prize unless they follow the rules. And hardworking farmers should be the first to enjoy the fruit of their labor" (2 Timothy 2:3-6 [NLT]).

We can view suffering in this world as symbolically compared with being a soldier at war in a foreign country, as the believer's true home is Heaven. The believer in Christ is conducting spiritual warfare against the enemy of souls, Satan and his demonic forces. These attacks cause suffering that must be endured as preparation for heavenly ranking.

We see this succinctly described in the book of Ephesians:

> Be strong in the Lord and in his mighty power. Put on all of God's armor so that you will be able to stand firm against all strategies of the devil. For we are not fighting against flesh-and-blood enemies, but against evil rulers and authorities of the unseen world, against mighty powers in this dark world, and against evil spirits in the heavenly places.
>
> Therefore, put on every piece of God's armor so you will be able to resist the enemy in the time of evil. Then after the battle you will still be standing firm. Stand your ground, putting on the belt of truth and the body armor of God's

righteousness. For shoes, put on the peace that comes from the Good News so that you will be fully prepared. In addition to all of these, hold up the shield of faith to stop the fiery arrows of the devil. Put on salvation as your helmet, and take the sword of the Spirit, which is the word of God. (Ephesians 6:10-17)

Soldiers do not expect to have it easy. They know they're in the battlefield to wage war. They dodge bullets and bombs, and engage in hand-to-hand combat. They have to be on their guard every second to stay alive. The Christian believer also is a "soldier for the cross," as an old hymn rings: "Stand up, stand up for Jesus, you soldiers of the cross. Lift high His royal banner, it must not suffer loss. From victory unto victory, His army shall He lead, till all the foe is vanquished and Christ is Lord indeed."

The above passage from 2 Timothy 2:3-6 tells us to endure suffering, not only as a soldier, but also as an athlete.

Godly Suffering: Athletes and the Olympics

I wrote this book during the 2012 Summer Olympics, which took place in London. I listened to story after story on the news about Olympic athletes who had trained since childhood for competition in their sport.

Turning their backs on the carefree life of a normal childhood, they chose instead the life of a dedicated athlete. One in particular caught my attention: American swimmer Michael Phelps, who was competing in his fourth Olympics. He declared the 2012 Summer Olympics to be his final one. He has been in strict training for the last twenty years, between the ages of seven and twenty-seven. Can you even imagine what that means?

Remarkably, Phelps earned his record-breaking twenty-second Olympic medal, collecting eighteen gold, two silver, and two bronze medals. He has won a total of seventy-one medals in major international long-course competition.

> Phelps began swimming at the age of seven, partly because of the influence of his sisters and partly to provide him with an outlet for his energy. When Phelps was in the sixth grade, he was diagnosed with attention-deficit hyperactivity disorder (ADHD). By the age of 10, he held a national record for his age group, and Phelps began to train at the North Baltimore Aquatic Club under Coach Bob Bowman. More age group records followed and Phelp's rapid improvement culminated in his qualifying for the 2000 Summer Olympics at the age of 15 and

becoming the youngest male to make a U.S. Olympic swim team in 68 years. While he did not win a medal, he did make the finals and finished fifth in the 200-m butterfly. (4)

God compels each of His children to live for Him as if they were training for the "Spiritual Olympics." Their preparation includes spiritual disciplines such as prayer and fasting, Bible study, repentance, forgiveness, and a host of other biblical principles.

Suffering for God's Glory Produces a Heavenly Harvest

The apostle Paul compares the endurance needed for the Christian life to that of a farmer's (2 Timothy 2:3-6). A farmer sacrifices blood, sweat, and tears to raise the crops and livestock to earn his income and provide the world with food.

There is little time for him and his family to take weekends off or to go on long vacations. From dawn to dusk—and sometimes into the night—he works to keep everything running smoothly and productively. He has to keep the machinery in good repair to prepare the ground for planting, cultivating, and harvesting crops.

A farmer cannot go to sleep until every last animal is fed, every cow is milked, eggs are gathered, and fieldwork is done. Similarly, after the Christian enters heaven, he or she will enjoy the blessings of his or her labor. God's divine plan and purpose has been accomplished. Now he or she can participate in his or her eternal reward.

Concluding Remarks

Since I've been home, my living arrangements and caregivers are working out fine. I am keeping up with the doctor's orders and able to maintain my health as I cope with all the challenges of my disability.

I am blessed to spend high-quality time with my family and friends. I also attend a few local churches nearby where my wife and I participate in worship. We enjoy sharing with all the pastors on the various staffs and many members of each congregation.

As the president and founder of 'Til Healing Comes Ministries, I do my best to serve and share posts on its blog, communicate about disability concerns, promote resources, and speak at churches. When I came home from the rehab center/nursing home, I immediately began writing this book. I worked on it almost daily until it was completed and released almost one and a half years later. Check out our ministry website: thcmin.org.

I believe these suggestions will help you keep your footing as you travel down the bumpy road of life:

- Learn to roll with the punches. This idiom comes from boxing lingo: "Step back or to one side as you are being hit so you do not receive the full force of the attack."
- Lower your expectations. You don't have to be the "best" to be God's best.
- Realize life is not fair. Only God has the answers about why.
- Enjoy the not-so-little things in life: a sunny day, a baby's smile, a friendly hug, a hot fudge sundae!
- Don't wait for life to become smooth in order to be happy. You'll wait forever.
- Accept the challenges of life. They will make you stronger and sweeter.
- Spend time regularly worshipping God, studying His Word, and talking to Him in prayer.
- Remember God put you on the earth to be His ambassador of goodwill. Let your joy come from serving God and others.
- Give God the glory. It was His to begin with.

Long for that day when Jesus will say to you, "Well done, my good and faithful servant. You have been faithful over a little; I will make you faithful over much. Enter into the joy of your master" (Matthew 25:21).

****

And the God of all grace, who called you to his eternal glory in Christ, after you have suffered a little while, will himself restore you and make you strong, firm and steadfast. To him be the power forever and ever. Amen.

—1 Peter 5:10-11

References to quotes

Chapter 1

1. *Giesler, Dr. Norman, http://www.evidencefor christianity.org/primitive-monotheism-by-norman-l-geisler-ph-d/, an article online.* Christian Apologetics Journal, Volume 1, No.1, Spring 1998. Copyright, Southern Evangelical Seminary, 1998
2. Sproul, Dr. R. C., *http://www.ligonier.org/learn/articles/book-job/, an article online, Ligonier Ministries, 2007*

Chapter 2

1. MacDonald, James, *When Life is Hard*, Moody Publishers, 2009, p.55
2. MacDonald, James, *When Life is Hard* (p. 55). Moody Publishers, 2009, p.55
3. Zacharias, Ravi and Geisler, Norman L. *Who Made God?: And Answers to Over 100 Other Tough Questions of Faith*, Zondervan Publishers, 2009, chapter 2

Chapter 3

1. Horton, Stanley M., Menzies, William W., *Bible Doctrines: A Pentecostal Perspective*, Logion Press, Springfield, MO, 1994, chapter 2
2. Chesterton, G. K. *Orthodoxy*, Re-Published by Popular Christian Publishing, 2010, chapter 5-Flag of the World
3. Lewis, C. S. *Mere Christianity*, HarperCollins Publisher, 1980. First published 1952, P. 47-48
4. http://www.brainyquote.com/quotes/authors/d/david_hume.html

Chapter 4

1. Strong's Concordance, #3804
2. Strong's Concordance, #3986
3. Pascal, Blaise, 1623-1662, a French mathematician, physicist, inventor, writer and Christian philosopher.
4. Scheibner, Steve "In My Seat: A Pilot's Story from Sept. 10-11" (2001) by Megan Scheibner, Zondervan Publishing 2012
5. Dickens, Charles "*A Christmas Carol*"

Chapter 5

1. http://www.addeigloriam.org/stories/morrison.ht
2. Zacharias, Ravi, *Has Christianity Failed You?*, Zondervan Publishers, 2010, Chapter 3

Chapter 6

1. Stevenson, Mary, *Footprints in the Sand*, 1936
2. White, James Emery, *A Traveler's Guide to the Kingdom: Journeying Through the Christian Life, Inter Varsity Press, 2012*, p. 17
3. Lewis, C. S, *The Problem of Pain*, HarperCollins Publisher, 2001, pgs. 91, 94
4. Fee, Gordon Dr., *The First Epistle to the Corinthians, The New International Commentary*, F. F. Bruce, General Editor (Grand Rapids: William B. Eerdmans Publishing Company, 1987 [reprint, 1993]), p. 536
5. davesgarden/guides/terms/go/712/
6. Winston Churchill, Prime Minister of England during WWII

Chapter 7

1. Wikipedia, s.v. Post-Polio Syndrome. http://en.wikipedia.org/
2. National Institute of Neurological Disorders and Stroke, http://www.ninds.nih.gov/disorders/post_polio/detail_post_polio.htm#204393172

Chapter 8

1. Check out this article on vehicle emissions of carbon monoxide. "Silent Shadow: Silent Killer,"

http://www.silentshadow.org/carbon-monoxide-in-your-car.html

2. Lucado, Max, *Grace: More Than We Deserve, Greater Than We Imagine*, Nashville, Tennessee, Thomas Nelson Publishers, 2012, p. 98

Chapter 9

1. Footnotes in the New International Version state that verse four in John 5:4 was added in some manuscripts to explain why the sick came to that particular pool.
2. Quote from James Emery White, Church and Culture Newsletter.
3. "Even If," written by Tony Wood and Scott Krippayne, Performed by Kutless
4. Mike Huckabee, Commentator for Fox News, http://www.christianpost.com/news/huckabee-clarifies-remarks-about-newtown-shooting-and-god-in-schools-86739/

Chapter 10

1. White, James, Emery, A Traveler's Guide to the Kingdom: Journeying Through the Christian Life, Intervarsity Press (2012)
2. Owen, John, *The* Biographical Dictionary of Evangelicals, p. 494
3. Owen, John, The Glory of Christ, Eremitical Press, (2009)

4. Brainerd, David, Biography is on *Wikipedia,* http://en.wikipedia.org/

5. Edwards, Johnathan, *The Life and Diary of David Brainerd*, Hendrickson Publishers

6. Bonar, Andrew, *Robert Murray M'Cheyne (McCheyne, alternate spelling) The Banner of Truth Trust,* 2012. First published 1844.

7. Keith Green, http://www.lastdaysministries. org/; Rich Mullin, http://www.kidbrothers.net

Chapter 11

1. 90 Minutes in Heaven, by Don Piper, on Revell, a Division of Baker Publishing, 2004

2. Heaven Is for Real, by Todd Burpo, Lynn Vincent, on Thomas Nelson Publishing, Nashville, TN 2011

3. Bruce, F. F., *The New Testament Documents: Are They Reliable?* Wm. B. Eerdmans Publishing Company, 2003 (See this book for further study on the reliability of the New Testament)

4. The Case for the Resurrection, by Lee Strobel, Zondervan Publisher, 2009, p. 55

5. Quote from the Audio Book by Randy Alcorn, *Life Promises for Eternity* http://www.epm.org/ blog/2012/Apr/23/anticipating-what-god-has-promised-life-promises-e

Chapter 12

1. A Tweet from Dr. John Piper (August 23, 2012)
2. "Bema" is the Greek word for the seat the judges sat on for athletic competition.
3. Max Lucado commented on suffering in one of his "Up-Link" online devotional messages.
4. Wikipedia, s.v. Michael Phelps. http://en.wikipedia.org/

Discussion Questions and Reflections— Chapter by Chapter

Chapter 1: Knocking on Heaven's Door

1. Share about a time when you experienced an unexpected illness.
2. How did it affect your faith in God?
3. Describe how Ken dealt with his life threatening circumstances.
4. Can you practically apply Philippians 1:20-26 and Romans 8:28 to your life? In what ways?
5. To what aspects of Job's life can you relate?

Chapter 2: Why, God?

1. What is it about suffering that causes people to ask why?
2. Discuss the positive and negative effects suffering can bring to your life.
3. If God's reason for allowing suffering into our lives is to cause us to ask the right questions, what are some of those questions?
4. What do these scriptures reveal about the origin of suffering: Genesis 1:31, Genesis 2:15-17 and Genesis 3:1-7, 17-19?

5. Expand on what Romans 1:24-32, Romans 3:23, Romans 6:23 and Romans 8:18-23 tell us about the results sin brought into the world.

Chapter 3: A Theology about Suffering

1. How is the Trinity revealed in Matthew 3:16-17? Explain the different functions for which each member of the Godhead is responsible.
2. According to Isaiah 53:2-6 and Hebrews 4:15-16, describe how Jesus suffered as the Messianic "Suffering Servant."
3. Explain how your relationship and bond can become stronger with Christ knowing He can relate to your suffering.
4. Why did God create human beings with a free will? How did that contribute to suffering entering the world?
5. How do free will and faith work together in the salvation process? (See Ephesians 2:8-10)

Chapter 4: The Value of Suffering

1. What does it mean to "share in the sufferings" of Christ?
2. Read 1 Corinthians 10:13 and explain what Paul means when he says, "God will never give you more than you can handle."
3. Discuss and put into your own words the quote from Christian philosopher Blaise Pascal who

said, "In faith there is enough light for those who want to believe and enough shadow for those who don't." (See page 72)

4. Share instances in Paul's life when God used suffering to discipline him and keep him humble. (See 2 Corinthians 11:23-12:10)
5. How has God used suffering to discipline or humble you and has it brought you closer to or further from Him?

Chapter 5: Overwhelming Odds

1. Describe a few of Ken's experiences in the nursing home.
2. If you or anyone in your family has spent time in a nursing home, share that experience.
3. Do you believe life is fair, why or why not? (See Isaiah 55:8-9, Ecclesiastes 9:11)
4. Explain what it means to be an ambassador for Christ and how that prepares someone to handle suffering? (See 2 Corinthians 5:20)
5. In what ways can suffering give a believer the opportunity to share his/her faith in Christ? (See Philippians 1:12-18)

Chapter 6: The Meaning of True Happiness

1. What is the difference between happiness and joy?

2. Describe an "in-the-valley" experience through which you have journeyed.
3. Share the ways suffering can reveal God's glory in your life.
4. Why is it so difficult to thank God for imperfections, blemishes and disabilities?
5. Relate a time you knew you were being disciplined by God through suffering and trials.

Chapter 7: Looking Back

1. Describe one way contracting polio affected Ken's life.
2. To which of Ken's trials and sufferings can you relate?
3. People often say they want to be "normal." How would you define "normal?"
4. What can you learn from Ken's grandfather and his Titanic experience?
5. Can you think of any talents or qualities you have developed during lessons from hard times? In what ways have they helped you to cope?

Chapter 8: A Life Changing Experience

1. If you have a personal relationship with God, what are some ways sufferings or difficulties have played a part in your spiritual development?
2. Invite the members of your group who haven't committed their lives to Christ yet, to do so now.

(See Romans 10:8-10,17) Lead them in a prayer of commitment. (See page 158)

3. How do you think losing a family member by a tragedy would affect your life and family?
4. Read Romans 8:28 and discuss how the truths of this verse made an impact on Ken and his family.
5. Have you been able to lead anyone to experience a personal relationship with Jesus Christ? Share the details.

Chapter 9: Don't Waste Your Suffering

1. Have you ever prayed for someone who is sick or suffering?
2. Discuss what Ken learned about divine healing and prayer for the sick.
3. Have you ever sensed God's presence with you during a tough and challenging time?
4. Why do you think God tells us to thank Him when trials come into our lives? (See James 1:2-5)
5. What lessons do you think Ken learned from his many falls?

Chapter 10: Arriving Home

1. Have you ever been away from home for an extended time? Describe what it was like for Ken to come home from the rehab center. Can you relate to this in any way?

2. Read 2 Corinthians 1:1-11 and discuss ways you can encourage and comfort others by sharing how God may have helped you deal with a trial, challenge or suffering.

3. What does the Bible tell us to do about fear and anxiety? (See 1 Peter 5:7-8, Philippians 4:6-8)

4. Discuss what Roman's 8:31-39 says about overcoming suffering.

5. How do Christian martyrs and faithful followers of Christ inspire you? Can you name a few?

Chapter 11: A Glimpse of Heaven

1. Discuss how the assurance of seeing Christ and your loved ones who are with Him in Heaven can minimize your fear of dying.

2. What does Hebrews 11:32-40 tell us about life's unfairness? How will God's amazing grace be the great equalizer in Heaven? (See 234-235)

3. Do you believe people can have near death experiences and come back to describe Heaven? Does it make any difference to your faith in Christ?

4. How does Jesus' bodily resurrection confirm a person's belief in Jesus and Heaven? (See 1 Corinthians 15: 3-11, Revelation 1:12-18)

5. How does Revelation 21:1-4 describe what Heaven will be like?

Chapter 12: The Hierarchy of Heaven and Activities
        Beyond

1. Refer back to pages 259-264 and discuss the possible rewards, rankings and responsibilities God will give to His children in Heaven.

2. What rewards or crowns do you hope to receive in Heaven? (See pages 264-269).

3. Why do you believe God will give various crowns and rewards to His children in Heaven?

4. If God uses this life on earth as a "boot camp," describe how the spiritual armor in Ephesians 6:10-18 is essential to prepare us for our heavenly life.

5. Are you confident when you meet Jesus in Heaven He will say "Well done my good and faithful servant?" If you are, explain why; if not, what can you do to be sure? (Matthew 25:21)

Scriptures Used–
Chapter by Chapter

Chapter 1: Philippians 1:20-26, Job 1:12, Job 2:9-10, Job 1:20-22, Job 13:15, Job 23:10, Job 42:10-17, Romans 8:28, Proverbs 3:5-6, Luke 4:4

Chapter 2: Matthew 16:26, Luke 12:15, Romans 1:2, Psalm 19:1, Romans 2:14, Genesis 1:31, Genesis 2:15-17, Romans 3:23, Genesis 3:1-7, Genesis 3:17-19, Romans 8:18-25

Chapter 3: Genesis 2:24, Ephesians 5:31-32, 1 Corinthians 6:15-17, 1 Corinthians 12:11-13, Revelation 13:8, Genesis 1:26, Genesis 11:7 (ESV), Matthew 19:5, Matthew 3:16-17, 28:19, John 1:14, Matthew 3:16-17, Matthew 28:19, John 1:29, Isaiah 53:2-6, Acts 8:27-39, 1 Peter 2:19-25, Matthew 27:46, Psalm 27:1, Hebrews 4:15-16, Isaiah 52:14, Colossians 1:24, Acts 8, Luke 24:13-35, Revelation 3:20, Acts 26:17-18, Acts 28:27, John 6:44, Acts 16:14, Romans 10:17, Romans 2:12-16, Luke 12:48, 1 Kings 19:12

Chapter 4: Romans 5:3, Romans 8:17-18, 2 Corinthians 1:5-7, Philippians 3:10, 1 Thessalonians 1:6, 2 Thessalonians 1:5, 1 Timothy 1:8, 1 Corinthians 10:13, Hebrews 11:1, Psalm 30:5, 2 Corinthians 12:7-10, Corinthians 12:7-10, Matthew 11:28-30, Revelation 21:4,

2 Corinthians 5:17, 1 Timothy 1:12-14, 1 Peter 1:6-8, Isaiah 48:10, John 16:33, Acts 14:22, Psalm 34:17-18

Chapter 5: 2 Peter 3:8 (ESV), Genesis 18:25, Psalm 115:3, Deuteronomy 29:29, Isaiah 55:8-9, Ecclesiastes 9:11, Daniel 3:16-18, Daniel 6:19-23, Isaiah 55:8, 2 Corinthians 5:20, 1 Peter 2:11, Philippians 1: 12-18, Philippians 1:29, Philippians 2:25-30, Philippians 4:4

Chapter 6: John 17:11-12, 24, Matthew 22:39-40, Psalm 22:1, Psalm 27:1, Matthew 27:6, Matthew 26:39, 1 Corinthians 13:12 (ESV), Psalm 119:105 (ESV), John 9:1-7, Exodus 32:25-35, Psalm 139:13-14, Exodus 4:11, Philippians 4:13, Nehemiah 8:10, Ps. 106:13-15, Psalm 107:20, Psalm 119:67, 1 Corinthians 11:23-30, Hebrews 12:7-13, 2 Peter 3:9, 1 Peter 4:19, John 15:1-4, Proverbs 23:10, Luke 7:18-19, 22-23

Chapter 7: Proverbs 3:5-6, Philippians 3:14, Psalm 127:3-5

Chapter 8: Romans 10:9-10, Matthew 6:33, John 3:3-7, Romans 12:17-21, Ephesians 2:8-10, 2 Corinthians 12:9, Hebrews 12:2

Chapter 9: John 11:35, Exodus 15:26, Genesis 20:17, Exodus 23:25, James 5:13-17, John 5:1-9, Ephesians 1:13-14, Revelation 21:4, Genesis 37-50, Mark 4:38-39, Acts 16:25-26, Psalm 46:1-3, Isaiah 43:2, Jeremiah 29:11 (NLT), 1 Peter 5:10, James 1:2-5, Matthew 6:11, Exodus 16, John 6:39, 41, 58, 2 Corinthians 4:1-12

Chapter 10: Matthew 6:10, 26:42, Matthew 6:31-34, 2 Corinthians 1:3-11, Hebrews 11:6, Galatians 3:11, Ephesians 2:8, Luke 12:25-26, 1 Peter 5:7, Proverbs 3:24, 1 Corinthians 6:19-20, Romans 5:8, Galatians 2:20, Psalm 34:17, Romans 8:31-39, John 14:1-6, Matthew 5:45, Matthew 7:24-27, Luke 16:22-25

Chapter 11: Psalm 23:4, Hebrews 11:32-40, Romans 8:18, 1 Corinthians 4:16-18, Hebrews 12:1-2, Mark 8:36, John 3:16, John 10:28, John 10:14, 27, John 5:28, John 11:38-44, Acts 14:19-20, Luke 16:19-31, Matthew 9:23-26, Acts 9:40-42, 2 Corinthians 12:2-6, Revelation 1 and 4, Mark 9:2-8, Mark 16:1-7, John 8:52, John 11:25, Luke 23:40-43, Philippians 1:21, 23, Acts 7:54-60, Acts 9:1-7, 2 Corinthians 12:1-4, 1 John 1:1-4, 1 Corinthians 15:3-8, Hebrews 10:27-28, 1 Corinthians 15:20, 1 Corinthians 15:54-57, Psalm 19:1-4, Psalm 19:1-4, Revelation 21:10-27, Ephesians 1:13-14, Ephesians 3:20, Colossians 3:1, Hebrews 11:16, Romans 8:20-25

Chapter 12: Revelation 21:1-3, 2 Timothy 4:6-8, Revelation 2:10, Matthew 25:14-15, 19-30, 1 Peter 3:22, Psalm 99:1, Isaiah 6:2, 9, Jude 1:9, Matthew 18:10, Ephesians 6:12, 1 Corinthians 9:24-27, 1 Corinthians 3:10-15, Matthew 25:31, 2 Timothy 2:12, Romans 5:17, Ephesians 5:25-32, Revelation 19:7, 1 Corinthians 12:29, 2 Corinthians 4:17, 2 Corinthians 4:16-18 (MSG), 2 Timothy 2:3-6 (NLT), Ephesians 6:10-17, Matthew 25:21

Recommended Reading

Alcorn, Randy, *Heaven,* Tyndale House Publishers, 2004

Alcorn, Randy, *If God Is Good: Faith in the Midst of Suffering and Evil*, WaterBrook Multnomah, 2009

Billheimer, Paul E. *Destined for the Throne: How Spiritual Warfare Prepares the Bride of Christ for Her Eternal Destiny*, Bethany House Publisher, 2005

Billheimer, Paul E. *Don't Waste Your Sorrows,* Bethany House, 2006

Bridges, Jerry, *Trusting God: Even When Life Hurts*, Nav Press, 2008

Lewis, C.S. *The Problem of Pain,* and *Mere Christianity,* HarperCollins Publisher, 1980

MacDonald, James When Life is Hard," by, Moody Press. 2009

Piper, John, and Taylor, Justin, *Suffering and the Sovereignty of God*, Crossway Publishing, 2006

Spurgeon, Charles, *The Suffering of Man and the Sovereignty of God*, Fox River Press, 2001

Tada, Joni Eareckson. *A Place of Healing: Wrestling with the Mysteries of Suffering, Pain, and God's Sovereignty*, Kingsway Communications Ltd, 2010

Tchividjian, Tullian Glorious Ruin: How Suffering Sets You Free, David C. Cook Publishing, 2012

Recommended Song List
for Inspiration

"Blessings" by Laura Story

"Come As You Are" by Pocketful of Rocks

"Even If" by Kutless

"I Can Only Imagine" by MercyMe

"I Lift My Hands" by Chris Tomlin

"Live Like That" by Sidewalk Prophets

"Steady My Heart" by Kari Jobe

"Strong Enough" by Matthew West*

"Survivors" by Matthew West

"Sweetly Broken" by Jeremy Riddle

"The Hurt and the Healer" by MercyMe

"Where I Belong" by Building 429

*Two Albums by Matthew West are dedicated to the stories of many who have suffered and faced great odds. "Into the Light" is a CD by Matthew West; specific songs on the album, "We Are the Broken," "Wonderfully Made," and "Moved by Mercy"- The other CD is "The Story of Your Life" by Matthew West; specific songs on the album, "Strong Enough," "Survivors."

Contemporary Christian Music moves me tremendously and assists my prayer and devotional life greatly. If you have a favorite listening device I encourage you to get a copy of these songs and set up a playlist that will go through these twelve songs one after the other. I hope it will encourage you to fight the good fight of faith and draw closer to God.

About the Author

K en Dignan is a credentialed minister, having been licensed to preach in 1976 and ordained in 1978. He has served in full-time vocational ministry since 1976 and has spent the majority of his career in pastoral offices in five churches. He helped lead two churches through solid growth and building programs. Offices he has held range from youth pastor to Christian education director, assistant pastor, and senior pastor. He has earned a bachelor's degree from North Central University (Mpls.MN) and a master's degree from the Assemblies of God Theological Seminary (Spfld.MO) both in Biblical studies.

Besides his pastoral ministry he founded a non-for-profit organization called 'Til Healing Comes Ministries in 1991. He produced and hosted a contemporary Christian radio program in the St. Louis area. He produced and hosted a thirty-minute weekly Christian television program aired on what was formerly known as TV38, WCFC in Chicago, TLN (Total Living Network) Comcast Cable, FamilyNet, and worldwide through satellite. He's a musician and singer, having released a gospel CD. He is an author, publishing a number of books available on Amazon.com or directly from 'Til Healing Comes Ministries, www.thcmin.org.

Ken is an avid sports fan, especially for teams in Chicago, loves music and good films.

He and his wife, Joni, are the parents of four sons—Andrew (wife Jodi), Patrick (wife Jennifer), the late Ryan (September 15, 1982-December 14, 2002), and Britt Stephen—and have two granddaughters.

Ken is currently serving as the director and founder of 'Til Healing Comes Ministries, along with being the pastor-at-large and writer for the Lift Disability Network. He is often a guest speaker at churches and various meetings.

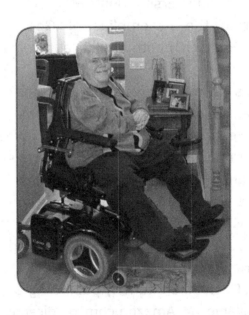